Peter Hardeman Burnett

The American Theory of Government Considered with

Reference to the Present Crisis

Peter Hardeman Burnett

The American Theory of Government Considered with Reference to the Present Crisis

ISBN/EAN: 9783337379599

Printed in Europe, USA, Canada, Australia, Japan

Cover: Foto ©ninafisch / pixelio.de

More available books at **www.hansebooks.com**

THE AMERICAN

THEORY OF GOVERNMENT

CONSIDERED

WITH REFERENCE TO THE PRESENT CRISIS.

BY

PETER H. BURNETT.

"I had rather be right than be President."—HENRY CLAY.

NEW YORK:

D. APPLETON & CO., 443 & 445 BROADWAY.

LONDON: 16 LITTLE BRITAIN.

1861.

exhibited, a second time, the beautiful novelty of a grea people voluntarily agreeing as to their condition anc wants, and calmly adopting a remedy for existing evils, " without having wrung a tear or a drop of blood from mankind." But regrets for the past are now wholly un-availing, and we must confront the stern facts as they are, and think and act *in* the "living present," but *for* the great future. We should, at as early a day as practica-ble, "turn a calm and scrutinizing eye" upon ourselves, "carefully examine the extent of the evils," ascertain the proper remedy, and willingly and promptly adopt it.

Having bestowed some attention and thought upon this subject, the writer submits the following views to the public, in the hope that they may be, to some extent, useful in their ultimate results. Though plainly and boldly stated, they are given with a kind and generous intent; and are addressed to all who love their country, and seek to promote its true and permanent interests.

CONTENTS.

CHAPTER I.

VALUE OF THE UNION.

CHAPTER II.

CAUSES OF THE CRISIS.

CHAPTER III.

THE ULTIMATE REMEDY.

THE

AMERICAN THEORY OF GOVERNMENT.

CHAPTER I.

VALUE OF THE UNION.

"It is of infinite moment that you should properly estimate the immense value of your national Union to your collective and individual happiness."—WASHINGTON.

§ 1. *Devotion to the Union should be based on sound reasoning.*

THE acute Calhoun, in that memorable speech, (the last one of any importance delivered by him in the Senate,) in speaking of the former union between the parent country and her colonies, very justly said :

"Washington was born and grew up to manhood under that union. He acquired his early distinction in its service, and there is every reason to believe that he was devotedly attached to it. But his devotion was a rational one. He was attached to it not as an end, but as a means to an end."

It may with equal truth be said, that the devotion of "the illustrious Southerner, whose mortal remains repose on the banks of the Potomac," to the present Union, "was a rational one;" for, unless the Union be intrinsically valuable "as a means to an end," it is unworthy of our love and respect, and should not and cannot be permanently sustained. And Mr. Calhoun was equally right, when he said in the same speech :

"It cannot, then, be saved by eulogies on the Union, however splendid and numerous. The cry of 'Union, Union—the glorious Union!' can no more prevent disunion, than the cry of 'health, health—glorious health!' on the part of the physician, can save a patient lying dangerously ill."

The time has been when no estimate of the value of the Union need to have been made. All was then internal peace and fraternal love. But that time has passed away; and we are now in a great crisis—a severe trial—a conclusive test, and *must* meet it as best we may. If we should prove unequal to the task, and be unable to rise with the mighty occasion, the world will have ample reason to know that we are but a degenerate people, and false claimants of merits not our own. We should, then, under existing circumstances, calmly and justly estimate the true value of the Union, and the ultimate probable effects of a permanent dissolution when accomplished. We shall then be prepared to make the greater efforts to prevent that overwhelming misfortune; for the efforts of a people, like those of an individual, will be in proportion to the estimated magnitude of the end to be attained.

§ 2. *The object of Government, and the right to institute it.*

It may be proper, in this place, to remark, that the main blessings of government consist not so much in conferring affirmative good, as in preventing intolerable evils. The primary object of government is to protect individuals against each other, and the combined whole against foreign enemies. It is not expected that government should contribute to the support of individuals, but that they should contribute to the support of the government. Men, when they enter into political society, must give up a portion of their individual natural rights, and confer upon their governmental agents the power to afford them efficient individual and national protection in return for the rights thus surrendered, and the powers thus conferred. This protection is the *greater* good; otherwise government would not exist.

It may also be proper to state in this connection, that, as a general rule, each distinct people have the political right to determine from time to time the form and powers of their own government. This right, however, is vested in the combined whole, speaking through the majority as its proper organs, and not in each separate part, acting alone for itself; otherwise a part would be greater than the whole. But what constitutes a distinct people is often a very difficult question, which can only be determined by the circumstances of each particular case. No intelligible general rule can be laid down ; because nature herself has not, in most cases, distinctly marked the appropriate boundaries of empires.

§ 3. *The benefits of the Union in the past, a rational basis for estimating its benefits in the future.*

The benefits derived from the Union in the past have been too palpable to need proof. They are seen everywhere, on land and on sea, at home and abroad. Our progress, in all the elements of material greatness, has been unprecedented. It has surely been *sufficiently* rapid to satisfy reasonable minds. We know from *actual*, and not merely speculative proof, what we have already accomplished. Could the same success have been attained without the Union ? If not, can we reasonably expect to prosper in the future by dissolution ? The proper answer to this question will depend upon a just estimate of the circumstances now existing, and those that will probably arise in the future.

As the geographical position, and the natural resources of our country, will be the same in the future as in the past, the argument drawn from this fact to show that we are, in the nature of the case, but one people, will always remain substantially the same. If it be true that our country has been so favored by nature, as to render one government for the whole, the most beneficial for each and every part, then no *permanent* severance of the Union can be justified by mere *temporary* causes. Permanent effects should flow from permanent causes. Time will cure temporary evils ; and it is wiser to endure them, trusting to the future justice of our country, than to war against the laws of nature. Our separation from Great Britain was justified, not so much by the alleged oppressions of the parent country, as by the fact that we could not be properly governed as *one people*. Our distance from the seat of government beyond seas, and the extent and varied capacity of our own country to sustain a distinct and powerful nation, were ample and permanent reasons for a permanent separation.

§ 4. *Difficulty of designating the dividing line between the sections.*

As a dissolution is possible, we will suppose it accomplished for the sake of the argument only; and then estimate, as well as we can, the probable legitimate results that will flow from such a condition. In doing so, we pass over the difficulty of dividing the public property, this being a temporary evil that time could cure.

The geographical features of the country are such, that the difficulty of determining the line separating the sections would seem to be insuperable. If we suppose the line so drawn as to separate the free from the slave States, the two divisions would be separated by an arbitrary air line, easily crossed at all points, and run without the least regard to the natural features of the country. It would commence on the Atlantic shore and extend west, passing more than two thousand miles through a country generally fertile, of good surface for settlement, with sufficient timber and water, and capable of sustaining a dense population in immediate proximity to the line on both sides of it; thus dividing our territory into two long narrow strips, lying with their sides to each other. There being between the two sections no impassable mountain ranges, or other serious natural obstructions, the only practicable mode of preventing smuggling would be to have no tariff. To fortify such a line, so as to make invasion difficult, would be impossible. Besides, this arbitrary line severs the great natural arteries of commerce, connecting every part of the rich and extensive valley of the Mississippi with the Gulf of Mexico. The position of this line would be determined, not by the natural features of the country, but upon the basis of a social institution, which, in the natural progress of population, will not probably endure to the end of the present century in many of the States where it now exists.

§ 5. *Frequent wars would be the consequence of permanent dissolution.*

The people on both sides of this long line of division would be brought face to face; and, as they speak the same language, the excitable masses would understand the insults of each other.

Our present national patriotic songs would no longer be sung, but would become obsolete and be forgotten. Other patriotic songs, celebrating alternate victories and defeats of both sections, would take their places. How could peace be preserved between dense masses of population thus situated?

The truth of this position is shown by the experience of other nations. The States of South America are generally divided from each other by air lines; and, though the people are of the same mixed races, profess the same religion, speak the same language, and have substantially the same manners and customs, revolutions and desolating wars are very common among them. The main reason is their proximity to each other. Brazil and Chili form exceptions to this rule; and, while the government of the first is a monarchy and that of the second a republic, they are both prosperous. Brazil is practically separated from other States by vast uninhabited tracts of country; and her greater population, and preponderating power, give her additional security. Chili is separated from La Plata by the Andes on the east, and from Bolivia by a desert on the north.* Contiguous nations are always enemies. The history of the world shows this to be true. Before the union of Scotland and England, the two nations were nearly always at war. The effect of the union has been to prevent these frequent wars; and this is the main reason why it has proven of such immense benefit to both countries. The mutual advantages of the union all admit. (Hal-

---

* The population of Brazil is some 8,000,000. Navy in 1857 consisted of forty-two ships in active service. Total naval force in 1858, 4,600 men. Revenue in 1859, was 19½ millions of dollars. Expenditures 18 millions. "The soundness of the general financial condition of the country was made evident during the commercial panic in the latter part of 1857, when Brazil stood firm, while almost all other countries were drawn into the vortex of the crisis." (New Am. Cy., art. *Brazil.*)

The population of Chili in 1857 was 1,558,453. "The Chilians are not a long-lived people; pulmonary diseases, affections of the heart and liver, and epidemic dysentery prove fatal to great numbers, and reduce the average duration of human life there to a lower point than in more variable climates." "The climate, though so delightful, seems to predispose the inhabitants to apathy and indolence, the *dolce far niente* of Italy." "A large part of the soil of Chili is unproductive." "The Chilenos are more enterprising than the inhabitants of most of the South American States, and the planters and merchants often accumulate large amounts of property." The mercantile marine in 1848 was 105 vessels, tonnage 12,628. In 1858, 269 vessels, tonnage 62,209. Increase in ten years 164 vessels, and 49,581 tons. "The improvement of the people in intelligence, wealth, and social progress, has been rapid within the last six years." (Id., art. *Chili.*)

lam's Constitutional History, 675.) England and France are neighboring nations and hereditary enemies.

Besides these causes of war, there would exist others not to be overlooked or forgotten. The people inhabiting the free States of the valley of the Mississippi, would never rest satisfied while the mouths of that river were in the possession of a foreign power. From the delicate and intricate nature of the interests involved, no treaty stipulations could possibly avoid difficulties. One party would feel insecure under the consciousness that the other was master of all access by water to the ocean. This jealousy and fear would inevitably produce collisions.

§ 6. *These wars would be carried on by regular soldiers.*

Each section is threaded with railroads and telegraphic lines, and a large invading force could be concentrated at almost any point along the line, within three days' time. In the present advanced state of the world, no time is lost in sending orders, and very little in concentrating troops. Napoleon said war was the art of concentrating the greatest number of men at a given point within a given time. The knowledge of the science and art of war is so well diffused in this age, and the courage of disciplined troops of different nations is so nearly equal, that numbers generally prevail. The general history of battles within the present century will prove this to be true. Napoleon, in his first campaigns, was able to rout his enemies; but long before the close of his career, he could only drive them from the field in good order. In most of the great battles fought by him, the hostile forces were about equal.

When this Union shall have been permanently dissolved, each division will be compelled to keep a standing army as large as it can support. The weaker section would naturally seek compensation in superior discipline. This would lead to the permanent creation of a large standing army; and what one does, the other, in self-defence, would be compelled to do. It would not be safe or wise to rely upon militia to repel a sudden invasion. Men engaged in the peaceful pursuits of life must have time for consideration, and some discipline, before they can have confidence in each other, and possess courage to meet a disciplined foe. The weakness of a peaceful and unarmed community was fully shown by the raid of old John Brown.

The condition of things on the continent of Europe proves the correctness of these views. France has a standing army of some seven hundred thousand men. Prussia, Austria, and Russia, the same; while that of Great Britain does not exceed three hundred thousand, and only some sixty thousand of these are kept at home. Were it not for her vast colonial possessions, and her general interference with continental affairs, her standing army, in time of peace, need not to exceed a hundred thousand men. The reason is, that her territory cannot be invaded by land, and she has the control at sea. We are, while united, in a better condition, because a wide ocean lies between us and all other powerful nations. An invasion of our country, while united, would be idle, if not impossible. But when we are once divided, the condition of things is entirely changed, and our enemies are at our very doors, always ready and able to attack us; and we must, of necessity, be able at all times to meet them. A standing army of a reasonable size, is not an evil but a benefit; but one as large as a people can possibly sustain, is a most grievous burden. It takes too much from the industrial force of the country, gives rise to exorbitant taxation, and becomes dangerous to liberty.

§ 7. *The evils of war.*

The evils of war are not properly estimated by the great mass of men, because they are prone to see only its glories. History shows that, in general, the masses are the first to clamor for war, and the first to ask for peace. By sad experience they find out the dire effects of this destructive custom.

Aside from the terrible destruction of human life,* the effects of frequent wars, in a business and financial point of view, may

---

* The effect of the frequent wars among a portion of the States of South America has been to produce a great disparity between the number of the sexes. Lt. Gibbon, in his account of the exploration of the valley of the Amazon, under the direction of the Department of the Navy, speaking of the town of Santa Cruz, in Bolivia, says:

"The women are very pretty, and affectionate to their husbands. He chooses her from among *five*, there being about that number of women to one man in the town." (Vol. ii., p. 161.)

I know not the author of the following article, nor have I examined authorities to be appreciated by considering the present condition of the different powers of Europe. The plan of carrying on war by means of national loans, is of modern origin. The beginning of the national debt of Great Britain was occasioned by the war with Holland in 1672. (Hallam's Con. His., 452, note.) It was further increased by the nine years' unsuccessful war, which terminated at the peace of Ryswick, and much augmented by

prove the correctness of the statistics given; but they are substantially correct in so far as my own recollection of history has enabled me to judge:

HAVOC TO LIFE BY WAR.—It is difficult to conceive what fearful havoc this custom has made of human life. It has at times entirely depopulated immense districts. In modern, as well as ancient times, large tracts have been left so utterly desolate that a traveller might pass from village to village, even from city to city, without finding a solitary inhabitant. The war of 1756, waged in the heart of Europe, left in one instance no less than twenty contiguous villages without a single man or beast. The Thirty Years' War, in the seventeenth century, reduced the population of Germany from 12,000,000 to 4,000,000—three-fourths; and that of Wirtemberg from 500,000 to 48,000—more than nine-tenths! Thirty thousand villages were destroyed; in many others the population entirely died out; and in districts once studded with towns and cities, there sprang up immense forests.

Look at the havoc of sieges, in that of Londonderry 12,000 soldiers, besides a vast number of inhabitants; in that of Paris, in the 16th century, 30,000 victims of mere hunger; in that of Malplaquet, 34,000 soldiers alone; in that of Ismael, 40,000; of Vienna, 70,000; of Ostend, 120,000; of Mexico, 150,000; of Acre, 300,000; of Carthage, 700,000; of Jerusalem, 1,000,000.

Mark the slaughter of single battles—at Lepanto, 25,000; at Austerlitz, 30,000; at Eylau, 60,000; at Waterloo and Quatre Bras, one engagement, in fact, 70,000; at Borodino, 80,000; at Fontenoy, 100,000; at Arbela, 300,000; at Chalons, 300,000 of Attila's army alone; 400,000 Usipetes slain by Julius Cæsar in one battle, and 430,000 Germans in another.

Take only two cases more: The army of Xerxes, says Dr. Dick, must have amounted to 5,283,320; and, if the attendants were only one-third as great as is common at the present in Eastern countries, the sum total must have reached nearly six millions. Yet in one year this vast multitude was reduced, though not entirely by death, to 300,000 fighting men; and of these only 3,000 escaped destruction. Jenghiz-Khan, the terrible ravager of Asia in the 13th century, shot 90,000 on the plains of Nessa, and massacred 200,000 at the storming of Kharasm. In the district of Herat, he butchered 1,600,000, and in two cities with their dependencies, 1,760,000. During the last twenty-seven years of his long reign, he is said to have massacred more than half a million every year; and in the first fourteen years he is supposed, by Chinese historians, to have destroyed not less than eighteen millions—a sum total of 32,000,000 in forty-one years.

In any view, what a fell destroyer is war! Napoleon's wars sacrificed full six millions, and all the wars consequent on the French Revolution some nine or ten millions. The Spaniards are said to have destroyed in forty-two years more than twelve millions of American Indians. Grecian wars sacrificed 15,000,000; Jewish wars, 25,000,000; the wars of the twelve Cæsars, 30,000,000 in all; the wars of the Roman Empire, of the Saracens and the Turks, 60,000,000 each; those of the Tartars, 89,000,000; those of Africa, 100,000,000! "If we take into consideration," says the learned Dr. Dick, "the number not only of those who have perished through the natural consequences of war, it will not perhaps be overrating the destruction of human life, if we affirm that one-tenth of the human race has been destroyed by the ravages of war, and, according to this estimate, more than fourteen thousand millions of human beings have been slaughtered in war since the beginning of the world." Edmund Burke went still further, and reckoned the sum total of its ravages, from the first, at no less than thirty-five thousand millions.

the war of the grand alliance, commenced in 1702, for the succession to the crown of Spain.*

The immediate relief to the nation has led to the practice, in modern times, of creating national debts to defray the extraordinary expenses of war. What the ultimate result of such a practice may be, time alone can determine. But the amount of the national debts of the different countries of Europe has become so great, that it would seem almost impossible to increase them to any considerable extent. There must, in the nature of things, be a point beyond which the national credit cannot go ; and when that point shall have been reached, the nation will not only have to pay the expenses of new wars without the aid of further loans, but also, at the same time, pay the interest upon former loans, or repudiate. A resort to the latter alternative would effectually destroy the credit of the government, and lead to a discontinuance of the practice of national loans.

This practice of creating great national debts is a selfish one,

---

* " A war of nine years, generally unfortunate, unsatisfactory in its results, carried on at a cost unknown to former times, amid the decay of trade, the exhaustion of resources, the decline, as their sums give reason to believe, of population itself, was the festering wound that turned a people's gratitude into factiousness and treachery." (Hallam's Con. His., p. 565.) The historian, on page 564, gives a detailed description of the financial condition of England, showing that " public credit sank so low, that in 1696 it was hardly possible to pay the fleet and army from month to month, and a total bankruptcy seemed near at hand. . . . Certainly the vessel of our Commonwealth has never been so close to shipwreck as in this period."

The war of the Grand Alliance produced results about as exhaustive. " The kingdom had been impoverished by twenty years of uninterruptedly augmented taxation, the annual burdens being triple in amount to those paid before the Revolution. Yet amid these sacrifices, we had the mortification of finding a debt rapidly increasing, whereof the mere interest far exceeded the ancient revenues of the crown, to be bequeathed, like an hereditary curse, to unknown ages." (Id., 608.) Though England had not been invaded, such was the state of distress produced by war, that the " population was at best stationary." France had suffered more severely. (Id., 609) During " the hundred years' war " between England and France, (1337 to 1453,) the sufferings of both nations were great, but those of France much greater. Twice France was upon the eve of becoming a dependency of the English crown.

" The nation, exhausted by the long wars of William and Anne, recovered strength in thirty years of peace that ensued ; and in that period, especially under the prudent rule of Walpole, the seeds of our commercial greatness were gradually ripened. It was evidently the most prosperous season that England had ever experienced . . . . In the war of 1743, which, from the selfish practice of relying wholly on loans, did not much retard the immediate advance of the country, and still more after the peace of Aix-la-Chapelle, a striking increase of wealth became perceptible."—(Hallam's Con. His., 656.)

and of very doubtful utility. Besides the sore burdens entailed upon posterity to pay the annual interest, the practice encourages war, and leads to extravagance in public expenditures. The debt of Great Britain, in 1857, was some eight hundred millions of pounds sterling, and the annual expenses thereon some twenty-eight millions. In 1817 it was eight hundred and forty-eight millions. The debt has been reduced a few millions by the government taking advantage of the decline in the rate of interest. The debt of France, in 1859, was some seventeen hundred millions of dollars, and the annual charges thereon some one hundred millions. In 1814, it was only two hundred and forty millions. The enormous cost of war may be appreciated by the fact, that in the war with France, from 1793 to 1815, Great Britain increased her national debt from two hundred and thirty-nine to eight hundred and forty-eight millions of pounds sterling, the increase being about equal to three thousand millions of dollars. The population of Great Britain is some twenty-eight millions, and that of the United States some thirty-one millions; and yet the annual interest upon her national debt is nearly double the yearly expenses of the Federal Government in time of peace.[*]

We have escaped the frequent wars that have so much desolated Europe. This impunity has arisen from the advantages of our position. Although our fathers suffered many privations in the Revolution, they did not endure the extreme exhaustion

---

[*] " What are the chief sources of expense in every government? What has occasioned that enormous accumulation of debts with which several of the European nations are oppressed? The answer plainly is, wars and rebellions; the support of those institutions which are necessary to guard the body politic against these two most mortal diseases of society. The expenses of those institutions which relate to the more domestic police of a State, to the support of its legislative, executive, and judicial departments, with their different appendages, and to the encouragement of agriculture and manufactures, (which will comprehend almost all the objects of State expenditure,) are insignificant in comparison with those that relate to the national defence. In the kingdom of Great Britain, where all the ostentatious apparatus of monarchy is to be provided for, not above one-fifteenth part of the annual income of the nation is appropriated to the class of expenses last mentioned, the other fourteen-fifteenths are absorbed in the payment of the interest of debts contracted for carrying on the wars in which that country has been engaged, and in the maintenance of fleets and armies."
—(Hamilton, *Federalist*, No. 34, p. 160.)

It will be observed that these remarks were made by Hamilton before the enormous increase of the debt of England, arising from the twenty-one years' war with France, had occurred. They are, therefore, more just at this time than when they were made.

felt on the continent of Europe, particularly in France. Our country was new, rich in soil, and too extensive to be thoroughly overrun; and there was, consequently, little or no starvation. France contributed one-twentieth of her entire population during the times of Napoleon, and lost one million seven hundred thousand men upon the field of battle. One-twentieth of our entire population during the Revolution, would have given us an army of about one hundred and seventy-five thousand men, a greater number than we lost during that memorable period. In the late war with England our sufferings were comparatively slight. We lost but few men in comparison to our population, and expended but a small amount of treasure, creating a national debt so small that the country, without exorbitant taxation, was enabled to pay it off in some sixteen years after the close of the war in 1815. But before the termination of the present unhappy contest, our people may know, perhaps, the real miseries of war, and be capable of estimating, with tolerable accuracy, the legitimate results of a permanent dissolution of the Union. This will be but *one* of many wars that must result in the future from such a misfortune.

§ 8. *Effects of dissolution upon national credit.*

With a divided Union, each section being invadeable by land, the credit of each would be bad, and high interest upon national loans the necessary result. Great Britain can borrow money at three per cent., while France, and other powers on the continent, are compelled to pay from five to six. In the course of a few centuries, this disadvantage is severely felt. All the countries of Europe, invadeable by land, have been invaded within the present century; and several of them more than once. Each successful invasion costs the country invaded about the labor of a generation, and destroys, for the time at least, the ability to pay the interest upon its bonds. People who invest their funds in government loans, are generally persons who seek repose in retirement from business, and who desire a safe and certain income. If they obtain only a low rate of interest, they can manage to live within their income, when the interest is punctually paid. *Security*, not profit, is their primary object.

2

§ 9. *Effects of dissolution upon the investment of capital.*

A country, invadeable by land, is not an inviting field for the employment of large amounts of capital. Capitalists are men who examine carefully, and judge dispassionately. They seek a safe and permanent investment for their money. They are not generally speculative men. Taken as a whole, the soil of France is of superior quality ; and the productive part of it bears a larger proportion to the entire extent of the country than in most European States, being as 41 to 52 ; and yet the want of large capital has been severely felt in both manufactures and agriculture. (New Am. Cy., art. *France.*) This fact is but the legitimate result of her geographical position. The knowledge of the fact that a country is invadeable by land, that it has been invaded repeatedly, and (judging the future by the past) that it will be invaded again, will necessarily deter large capitalists from investments there so long as other opportunities, more safe, are available. It does not matter how brave and skilful the people of a country invadeable by land may be, there will arise, in the progress of human affairs, some untoward crisis, when a successful invasion can be made. Factions among the people, a weak, rash, or irresolute cabinet, superior talent at the head of a rival nation, and many other causes, may arise. Had England been invadeable by land, could her people, with all their conceded skill and valor, have resisted the army led by Napoleon against Russia ? A people thus situated always work under the dispiriting reflection that their country may be successfully overrun at any time, and the results of their industry either greatly impaired or totally swept away. During the Peninsular war, the factories of Spain were mostly destroyed by the military operations of the hostile forces.

The advantages of her position is the reason why the capital of the world is mainly concentrated in England. Capital is safer there than at any other *easily accessible* point. Hence the greatest houses, financial and commercial, are found there. Our country united possesses like advantages in respect, at least, to many portions of the globe. Capital has been steadily accumulating, and commerce and manufactures have increased in a corresponding degree. But let the Union be permanently severed, and the disastrous results will become, in due time, too palpable to be mistaken.

§ 10. *Dissolution fatal to supremacy at sea.*

No country, invadeable by land, can reasonably hope, at this late day, to become the leading naval power among the maritime nations of the earth. A people thus situated must, of necessity, keep up a large standing army, and cannot, therefore, support, at the same time, the most efficient navy in the world. These two burdens together would be more than any people could well bear.

Had the position of the French and English been reversed, the result of their rivalship on the sea might have been very different. As it was, the English had the more powerful motives to impel them to victory. They knew that, if successful, not only honor, but safety from invasion at home, would be the result. On the contrary, the French knew success at sea would still leave their country open to invasion by land; and that, therefore, the necessity for keeping up a large standing army would not be obviated.

United, we will be able, in the course of another century, if not sooner, to put afloat a navy equal, if not superior, to any on the ocean. But with a divided country, that great prospect vanishes.

§ 11. *Despotism the ultimate result of dissolution.*

It has long been the fixed opinion of the best English and American statesmen, that large standing armies are inimical to free government. Mr. Pulteney, as cited by Mr. Hallam, declared in 1732 that he " always had been, and always would be, against a standing army of any kind; it was to him a terrible thing, whether under the denomination of parliamentary or any other. A standing army is still a standing army, whatever name it may be called by; they are a body of men distinct from the body of the people; they are governed by different laws; blind obedience and an entire submission to the orders of their commanding officers is their only principle. The nations around us are already enslaved by those very means; by means of their standing armies they have every one lost their liberties ; it is, indeed, impossible that the liberties of the people can be preserved in any country where a numerous standing army is kept up."

The opposition to standing armies has often been carried to extremes. One of *reasonable size* is not dangerous to liberty, but necessary to security. It is true, that no government can be beneficially administered, unless it gives general satisfaction to at least a majority of the governing class, whatever that class may be ; but it is *equally* true, that no government can long rule by universal consent; and every practical government must, therefore, have the means to promptly put down mere factions, and to render revolution, in the beginning, difficult to minorities. A standing army, sufficient for this purpose, is necessary to every well-regulated State. The extreme right of revolution is very often abused. Masses of men are often governed by passion and not by reason. Suffering men must and will complain ; and from whatever cause these ills may arise, they are generally prone to attribute them to the government. The burdens of government are plainly seen and felt ; while its blessings " fall silently like the dews of heaven," and are often unseen or under-estimated by the governed.

The dangerous character of a large standing army arises from the nature and purposes of its organization. Strict discipline and ready obedience are absolutely necessary to military efficiency. There must be perfect unity in the organization, and the mighty mass must move as one man, impelled by a single will ; and, therefore, to secure this essential unity of action, the command can only be given to a single mind. This fact makes the government, whatever may be its form, a *practical* despotism. There may be a legislative body, and the people may be allowed to elect its members ; but they will not vote freely under the gigantic shadow of a large standing army ; and a majority of the members, when elected, will not oppose the determined will of the commander-in-chief. Until the army itself becomes demoralized, or the people come to the united and desperate resolution to risk all to carry their point, they will not even *begin* any serious opposition to the measures of government. The natural instincts of men will force them, under such circumstances, to side with power.

Mr. Gibbon, in summing up his views of the character of the imperial government of Rome, very justly remarks:

" To resume, in few words, the system of the imperial government, as it was instituted by Augustus, and maintained by those princes who understood their own interest and that of the people, it may be defined an absolute monarchy disguised by the forms of a commonwealth. The masters of the Roman world surrounded their throne with darkness, concealed their irresistible strength, and humbly professed themselves the accountable ministers of the Senate, whose supreme decrees they dictated and obeyed."—(*Decline and Fall*, chap. iii.)

§ 12. *The same subject continued.*

A permanent dissolution of the Union being accomplished, republican government would not only fail on this continent, but representative government, in any efficient form, could never be sustained. Despotism—the one-man power—would be the legitimate and inevitable ultimate result. It would be the only practical theory under the circumstances. Government must be practical to be government at all. The theory may be beautiful to the imagination, but unless strictly practical, it must fail to accomplish the very end intended by its institution.

The practical efficiency of a governmental theory depends upon its proper adaptation to the circumstances and geographical position of the country to be governed. A theory practical for one country, will not operate successfully in another differently situated. So, under a people practically free, the power over the purse and the sword of the nation must be placed in the hands of representatives *freely* chosen by the people themselves. In England, for example, no army can exist, and no money can be appropriated, without the consent of Parliament. Owing to her impunity from invasion, the Government can wait the sluggish movements of Parliament; but France, and other countries differently situated, cannot do this; especially in this fast age. When the country is invaded, and the national existence is in peril, it will not do to wait two months to elect a Speaker, and spend two months' time in debating over an appropriation bill. Action, prompt and united, must be had; and only the strongest form of government can secure it; for it is true, that "great armies, prompt obedience, unlimited power over the national resources, secrecy in council, rapidity in execution, belong to an energetic and enlightened despotism." (Hallam's Con. His., 460.) On the field of battle there must be but one commander-in-chief; and a country invaded is but a large battle-field. In such a case, it will not be safe to rely upon the action of deliberative bodies; because, in times of extreme peril, they are often factious or paralyzed.* This results from the known characteristics of the human mind, men being prone to differ in their views, and apt to be tenacious of their opinions, in proportion to the estimated importance of the subject to which they relate. During the existence of the Republic, the members of the Assembly were engaged in debating some abstract philosophical theory, while their enemies were invading France.

Hasty and prejudiced writers generally speak in disparaging terms of the despotic governments of Europe. Their objections are not well and thoroughly considered. The true fundamental cause is found in the necessities of their condition. The best statesmen on the continent know that the English representative theory never can be successfully carried out, except in countries substantially situated as England is. It has been repeatedly tried and as often failed. "It is not a new observation that the people of any country (if, like the Americans, intelligent and well-informed) seldom adopt, and steadily persevere for many years, in any erroneous opinions respecting their own interests." (Mr. Jay, *Federalist*, No. 3, p. 14.) The people of the different States of Europe are enlightened, and have had most ample time and opportunity to test the practical character of the differ-

---

* "Are not popular assemblies frequently subject to the impulses of rage, resentment, jealousy, avarice, and of other irregular and violent propensities? Is it not well known that their determinations are often governed by a few individuals in whom they place confidence, and that they are of course liable to be tinctured by the passions and views of those individuals? . . . . . Is it not time to awake from the deceitful dream of a golden age, and to adopt as a practical maxim for the direction of our political conduct, that we, as well as the other inhabitants of the globe, are yet remote from the happy empire of perfect wisdom and perfect virtue?"—(Hamilton, *Federalist*, No. 6, pp. 27 and 29.)

. . . "But popular, that is, numerous bodies, are always prone to excess, both from the reciprocal influence of their passions, and the consciousness of irresponsibility "—(Hallam's Con. His., 647.)

ent theories of government, and the conclusions of their best intellects upon this subject can hardly be erroneous.

It is the general opinion of writers upon the science of government, that a despotism is the strongest and most efficient. Time and common sense have proven this opinion to be true. In this form of government there is less security against oppression at home, and greater security against oppression from abroad. What theory a people should adopt, depends upon the question, which is the greater danger? In the Revolution, our greatest danger was from *abroad;* and, by making Washington a dictator, we saved our country. When that danger had passed away, we could well dispense with this energetic but despotic power. If the Union were divided, the same circumstances would compel the people of the different divisions to do the same thing; and as the danger from abroad would be immediate and permanent, the despotism must, of necessity, become permanent also. In the wars between the little States of South America, they confer dictatorial powers upon their Presidents; and though they are often blamed, it is by those who have not justly estimated the exigencies of their condition. It was the fear of invasion, that seems to have constituted one of the main reasons why the people of England submitted so readily to the despotic powers exercised by the Tudors and Stuarts. It was not the overshadowing influence of a standing army, as this was only begun under the reign of Charles II., and amounted in 1662 to only some 5,000 men, a very small force as compared to the standing armies of other European monarchies of that age.—(Hallam's Con. His., 411.)

United, we are in a better condition than England; because our position not only gives us like impunity from invasion, but exempts us, at the same time, from all pretences for entering into entangling foreign alliances, to preserve the balance of power. The practice of England in making war on the continent for this reason, has caused her very great sacrifices in blood and treasure. Her present enormous national debt is mainly the result of such wars.* Whether this practice on her

* We have already seen that the national debt of Great Britain was increased in twenty-one years' war with France, more than 600 millions of pounds sterling. At the commencement of that mighty struggle, her army was very small; and, from this cause, it was years before she could act on the continent with vigor. It has been contended by

part can be justified by wise statesmanship may admit of very
grave doubts. But let us sever and divide our country, and we
will be in a worse condition than the people on the continent
of Europe. There are many great natural features on that continent that mark the dividing lines between nations, making
defence more easy, and invasion more slow and difficult; and
the doctrine of the balance of power is there established, and a
weak State can exist, because the Great Powers will not tolerate
its conquest. In our country, we have no impassable moun-
tains, and there is here no doctrine of the balance of power
established, and the weaker State would be at the ultimate
mercy of the stronger. The people of the more powerful State
would, at last, come to the conclusion that their own safety and
the best ultimate humanity would justify the complete conquest
of their neighbor. There is every reason to believe, that, for
some time before the Union, the people of England had inflex-
ibly made up their minds to conquer Scotland. The people of
both countries had been so long harassed and impoverished
by their frequent wars, that the patience of both must have
been well nigh exhausted. It had often required the utmost
exertions of the Scots to sustain themselves. (Hallam's Con.
His., 675.) From the geographical features of our country,
and its position on the globe, it would seem that the Almighty
never intended it to be divided.*

able writers, that it is the better and more economical policy of that kingdom to keep
up a standing army of at least medium size.

"In the late war, the inability of Great Britain to act from the first with vigor,
compelled her to fight twenty-one years, with incalculable waste of blood and treasure,
merely to restore the balance of power; and the nation, which at first had only three
battalions for service, ended, in 1814, with a mass of more than a million of men in
arms."—(En. Brit., art. *War*, p. 736.)

* "This country and this people seem to have been made for each other, and it
appears as if it was the design of Providence, that an inheritance so proper and convenient for a band of brethren, united to each other by the strongest ties, should never
be split into a number of unsocial, jealous, and alien Sovereignties."—(Jay, *Federalist*,
No. 2, p. 12.)

"The world may politically, as well as geographically, be divided into four parts,
each having a distinct set of interests. Unhappily for the other three, Europe, by her
arms and by her negotiations, by force and by fraud, has, in different degrees, extended
her dominion over them all. Africa, Asia, and America have successively felt her
domination. The superiority she has long maintained, has tempted her to plume herself as the mistress of the world, and to consider the rest of mankind as created for her
benefit. Men, admired as profound philosophers, have, in direct terms, attributed to

§ 13. *A despotism inimical to a free press.*

It would seem impossible, in the very nature of things, that a free press should ever exist under a despotism, for two reasons:

1. The attacks of the press are levelled against a single individual; and there are but few persons who would singly bear the attacks of the press, when they have the power to restrain them. It is not in human nature.

2. The safety of the government itself would require restrictions upon the press. Though a despotism may be the very best practical government for a country invadeable by land, and situated in the vicinity of neighbors sufficiently powerful to give serious trouble; yet such is the restlessness of dense populations, that they are prone to see only results, while they overlook their causes. A free press in a despotism would be constantly making disparaging comparisons between the condition of the people at home, and that of the people living under a free government abroad; while the true cause of this difference would be carefully concealed, and the masses unjustly excited against their own government. The difference in the amount of freedom enjoyed would be palpable, but the cause of that difference would be misrepresented, and the public censure would fall upon the government. Superficial and prejudiced reasoners are almost certain to assign the wrong cause for the known effect.

§ 14. *Dissolution exposes us to foreign aggression.*

This chapter will be concluded with the following forcible extract from the forty-first number of the *Federalist* by Mr. Madison.*

her inhabitants a physical superiority; and have gravely asserted, that all animals, and with them the human species, degenerate in America; that even dogs cease to bark, after having breathed awhile in our atmosphere.* Facts have too long supported those arrogant pretensions of the European; it belongs to us to vindicate the honor of the human race, and to teach that assuming heathen moderation. Union will enable us to do it. Disunion will add another victim to his triumphs."—(Hamilton, *Federalist*, No. 11, p. 57.)

* The reader is referred to the Appendix, containing the sixth and eighth numbers of the *Federalist*, by Hamilton. The reason for their republication in this form is, that

Recherches philosophiques sur les Americains.

"The Union itself, which the Constitution cements and secures, destroys every pretext for a military establishment which could be dangerous. America united, with a handful of troops, or without a single soldier, exhibits a more forbidding posture to foreign ambition, than America disunited with a hundred thousand veterans ready for combat. It was remarked, on a former occasion, that the want of this pretext had saved the liberties of one nation in Europe. Being rendered by her insular situation, and her maritime resources, impregnable to the armies of her neighbors, the rulers of Great Britain have never been able, by real or artificial dangers, to cheat the public into an extensive peace establishment. The distance of the United States from the powerful nations of the world, gives them the same happy security. A dangerous establishment can never be necessary or plausible as long as they continue a united people. But let it never for a moment be forgotten, that they are indebted for this advantage to their union alone. The moment of its dissolution will be the date of a new order of things. The fears of the weaker, or the ambition of the stronger States or confederacies, will set the same example in the new as Charles VII. did in the old world. The example will be followed here from the same motives which produced universal imitation there. Instead of deriving from our situation the precious advantage which Great Britain has derived from hers, the face of America will be but a copy of that of the continent of Europe. It will present liberty everywhere crushed between standing armies and perpetual taxes. The features of disunited America will be even more disastrous than those of Europe. The sources of evil in the latter are confined to her own limits. No superior powers of another quarter of the globe intrigue among her rival nations, inflame their mutual animosities, and render them the instruments of foreign ambition, jealousy, and revenge. In America, the miseries springing from her internal jealousies, contentions, and wars, would form a part only of her lot. A plentiful addition of evils would have their source in that relation in which Europe stands to this quarter of the earth, and which no other quarter of the earth bears to Europe.

the present edition of that work seems to have been exhausted, and copies are difficult to be had. It is well to often recur to this mine of wisdom, and especially at this period.

"This picture of the consequences of disunion cannot be too highly colored, or too often exhibited. Every man who loves peace; every man who loves his country; every man who loves liberty, ought to have it ever before his eyes, that he may cherish in his heart a due attachment to the Union of America, and be able to set a due value on the means of preserving it."

CHAPTER II.

CAUSES OF THE CRISIS.

§ 1. *Causes of the Crisis stated.*

VARIOUS causes have been assigned by our public men, and by the press, for the present unhappy condition of the country; all of which have doubtless had their influence. Some attribute it to the agitation of the slavery question; others to disappointed party and sectional ambition; and others to the general corruption of our politicians. But the true fundamental cause lies much deeper; and is to be found in the *theory of our government.* All others are but *secondary* causes; and constitute, in fact, only different *tests* of the theory, as did the tariff question of 1833.

A true theory will vindicate, and a false theory betray itself, sooner or later. Every man in the nation may enthusiastically support an erroneous theory of government in the beginning; and yet time will assuredly show its fallacy. The eternal and inflexible laws of logic can no more be violated with impunity than the laws of nature. Man is but a *subordinate* being, and cannot lift himself above the laws of truth. If he attempts to do so for the time being, his ultimate fall will be only the more painful in proportion to the extent and duration of his transgression.

The fundamental vice in our theory, is the attempt to divide, between the Federal and State Governments, that supreme element or principle which we call sovereignty—a thing, in its very nature, indivisible.* In reference to the powers conferred upon the Federal Government, we are *one* people; but in regard to the powers reserved to the States, we constitute distinct and antagonistic communities; and the powers reserved to the States are *so great in amount,* and *so important in character,* that, by a simple abuse of these powers, the Union can be ultimately rendered intolerable; and the theory itself provides no efficient and peaceful remedy for the evil. The only remedy provided by the Constitution in reference to the abuse of the *reserved* powers, is found in the will of each State, and not in that of the combined whole.

By our theory, the citizen is made capable of committing treason, at one and the same time, against two separate and distinct sovereignties. This is a solecism in government. It is very true, that the theory assumes to clearly distribute the mass of duties to be performed by the citizen into two classes, and to assign one class to each sovereignty. It requires him to serve two distinct masters; but, at the same time, claims to give each master jurisdiction over him in different respects.

Another great vice in the theory, but subordinate, perhaps, to the other, is to be found in the number of *elective* officers, and the short duration of their terms. Our theory of government substantially requires more public and private virtue to sustain it, than any other; and yet its inevitable tendency is ultimately to undermine and subvert the very virtue upon which alone it can hope to live.

These may be justly considered very bold and summary positions. But are they not *true?* If true, they should be believed; if false, they should be unhesitatingly rejected; and

---

* In the case of Barron *v.* The City of Baltimore, Chief Justice Marshall, in delivering the opinion of the Court, said:

"The Constitution was ordained and established by the people of the United States for themselves; for their own government, and not for the government of the individual States. Each State established a Constitution for itself, and, in that Constitution, provided such limitations and restrictions on the powers of its particular government as its judgment dictated."

So, in the case of Ableman *v.* Booth, in December Term, 1858, (21 Howard, 516,) Chief Justice Taney, in delivering the unanimous opinion of the Court, said:

"And the powers of the General Government and of the State, although both exist and are exercised within the same territorial limits, are yet separate and distinct sovereignties, acting separately and independently of each other, within their respective spheres."

whether true or false, time will determine. These positions are stated without hesitation, and will be supported by the reasons hereinafter given, and others that will no doubt suggest themselves to the mind of the intelligent reader. It is the simple duty of every writer to be *honest*, and to *plainly* state that which he believes to be true, without regard to apprehended praise or censure.

But while these positions are thus plainly and boldly stated, it is done with all due and becoming respect for the views of others ; and especially for those of a great majority of the patriotic men, who took part in forming the Constitution. There is, however, the best reason to know, that the wisest of our statesmen of that day never did give our theory their entire approbation. They supported it, not as perfect, but as being better than the Articles of Confederation. It was considered by them as an experiment only. The authority of a *few* truly great minds is of more weight than that of *many* subordinate ones.

§ 2. *Circumstances under which the Constitution was framed and ratified.*

During the progress of the Revolution, and after the Colonies had declared their independence, impelled by the pressure of common dangers, sufferings, and hopes, the thirteen States entered into the Articles of Confederation. The circumstances of the times did not admit of mature deliberation.

Congress was the organ through which the Confederation spoke ; and in the passage of measures each State had one vote. These measures were addressed to organized communities, and not to the individuals of whom they were composed. Each State was bound to contribute its portion to the common treasury ; and this portion was based upon the value of all land within each State ; but the taxes necessary to raise the national revenue were to be levied and collected by each State. The vote of nine States was necessary to pass the more important measures ; such, for example, as related to war, treaties, coining money, and ascertaining the sums necessary for the defence and welfare of the United States. In the thirteenth and last article it was declared :

" Each State shall abide by the determinations of the United States in Congress assembled, on all questions which by this Confederation are submitted to them. And the articles of this Confederation shall be invariably observed by every State, and the union shall be perpetual; nor shall any alteration at any time hereafter be made in any of them, unless such alteration be agreed to by a Congress of the United States, and be afterwards confirmed by the legislatures of every State."

Notwithstanding the excellent dispositions of the people, and the strong pledges of inviolable fidelity contained in the Articles, the Confederation soon failed through its own weakness. In reference to this state of things, Hamilton, in the fifteenth number of the *Federalist*, has these forcible remarks:

" It has happened as was to have been foreseen. The measures of the union have not been executed; the delinquencies of the States have, step by step, matured themselves to an extreme, which has at length arrested all the wheels of the National Government, and brought them to an awful stand. Congress at this time scarcely possesses the means of keeping up the form of administration, till the States can have time to agree upon a more substantial substitute for the present shadow of a Federal Government. Things did not come to this desperate extremity at once. The causes which have been specified, produced at first only unequal and disproportionate degrees of compliance with the requisitions of the Union. The greater deficiencies of some States furnished the pretext of example, and the temptation of interest to the complying, or least delinquent States. Why should we do more in proportion than those who are embarked with us in the same political voyage? Why should we consent to bear more than our proper share of the common burthen? These were suggestions which human selfishness could not withstand, and which even speculative men, who looked forward to remote consequences, could not without hesitation combat. Each State yielding to the persuasive voice of immediate interest or convenience, has successively withdrawn its support, till the frail and tottering edifice seems ready to fall upon our heads, and crush us beneath its ruins."

The Convention assembled under very embarrassing circumstances. They had not only the difficult task to perform,[*] of forming a Constitution for a great country; but they had to do this by the union or merging of *independent sovereign States.* The members not only differed in their own views, but they had no power of *final* action; their province being very similar to that of a committee charged with drafting a bill upon a given subject, to be afterwards submitted to the House. The Constitution framed by the Convention, had to pass through the severe ordeal of the separate State Conventions; and by a provision of the seventh article, the ratification of nine States was necessary to give it effect; and then only. between the States so ratifying the same. This provision was in violation of the Articles of Confederation, by which the assent of all the States was required to make amendments. As all the States under the Confederation were sovereign, and the people had become accustomed to this independent equality, any proposition to reduce, either the importance of all, or the relative importance of the smaller States, would be certain to meet with the most determined opposition in the separate State Conventions.

Statesmen are not always able to do what they would; and they are, therefore, forced by circumstances, to either do nothing, or to do the best they can. The times were perilous, and the necessity for action most imperative; and the best minds in the Convention were so trammelled, and so compelled to act against their better judgment, that they were not able to accomplish as much, perhaps, as those of inferior capacity, but whose views were made in harmony with State pride and local jealousy.

§ 3. *The same subject further considered.*

The fear that the Constitution would be rejected by the separate States, and of the great perils likely to follow such a

---

[*] In his disquisition on government, Mr. Calhoun has these just and forcible remarks:

"Instead of a matter of necessity, it is one of the most difficult tasks imposed on man to form a Constitution worthy of the name; while to form a perfect one—one that would completely counteract the tendency of government to oppression and abuse, and hold it strictly to the great ends for which it is ordained—has thus far exceeded human wisdom, and possibly ever will. From this another striking difference results. Constitution is the contrivance of man, while government is of Divine ordination. Man is left to perfect what the wisdom of the Infinite ordained as necessary to preserve the race."—(Works of Calhoun, vol. i., p. 8.)

misfortune, no doubt had a serious and often a controlling influence over the members of the Convention.* They knew that in each of the separate State Conventions, all the elements of opposition would have full scope for their exercise, and that a rejection by five States only would be *entire* defeat. In these separate State Conventions, State pride, local attachments, and an unreasonable dread of the loss of liberty, would effectually defeat any strong theory of government. The people of America had felt, more in anticipation than in practice, the unlimited powers claimed over them by the mother country. The masses had not had time to fully comprehend the true character of their changed condition. The powers which they had feared, were not only without limit, but they were exercised by a country beyond seas; in whose councils they had no representative voice, and the interests of whose people were widely different from, and even antagonistic to, their own. They had passed through *revolution*, and they were now placed in the *new* position of *re-organization*. During the progress of the Revolution, and for years before, they had been alone taught

---

* An examination of the proceedings of the Convention will show the influence which the fear of rejection exercised upon the minds of members. The plan of proceedings adopted by that body was for members to introduce their propositions in the form of resolutions. Edmund Randolph of Virginia, on the 29th May, 1787, (Journal, p. 68,) introduced a series of resolutions, and a part of the 6th resolution of this series gave Congress the power "to negative all laws passed by the several States, contravening, in the opinion of the national legislature, the articles of *union*, or any treaty subsisting under the authority of the Union." This proposition was agreed to, May 31, (Journal, 87.) Mr. Pinckney, of South Carolina, on the 6th of June, (Journal, 104,) gave notice of a motion for a reconsideration, which motion was not agreed to, June 8, (Journal, 107.) The resolutions of Mr. Randolph, as amended and agreed to, are given in full, (Journal 134,) and this clause is included in the words of the original. Afterwards the proposition was not agreed to by the following vote:

Yeas—Massachusetts, Virginia, and North Carolina - - - - - 3
Nays—Connecticut, New Jersey, Pennsylvania, Delaware, Maryland, South Carolina, and Georgia - - - - - - - - - - - 7

The testimony of M. Gouverneur Morris, upon whose motion the third section of the fourth article of the Constitution was introduced, is very strong. In a letter written in 1803, he said:

"In wording the third section of the fourth article, I went as far as circumstances would permit, to establish the exclusion. Candor obliges me to add my belief, that, had it been more pointedly expressed, a strong opposition would have been made."—(3 Mor. Wri., 192.)

It is not at all surprising that so many difficulties of construction have arisen, when those who framed the Constitution candidly admit, that the fear of opposition made them *purposely clothe their ideas in ambiguous terms.*

to *resist* power; but now they were called upon to bestow it upon their own Government. They did not seem to fully understand the fact, that *even* the *same powers* in their own Government would be less dangerous to *their* liberties, than in that of England. They had, very naturally, under the circumstances, an extreme dread of power. It was true, that the Confederation had most signally failed; but the old habits of thought and feeling were still powerful. An unreasonable confidence in human nature, and an exaggerated estimate of the capacity and fidelity of the States, was the great evil of that day, and has been ever since. The architects who framed the Constitution, were compelled to model the work according to the existing views of others.

The following extracts from the fifteenth number of the *Federalist*, by Hamilton, will place this subject in a clear and strong light:

"It is true, as has been before observed, that facts too stubborn to be resisted, have produced a species of general assent to the abstract proposition, that there exist material defects in our national system; but the usefulness of the concession, on the part of the old adversaries of federal measures, is destroyed by a strenuous opposition to a remedy, upon the only principle that can give it a chance of success. While they admit that the Government of the United States is destitute of energy, they contend against conferring upon it those powers that are requisite to confer that energy. They seem still to aim at things repugnant and irreconcilable; at an augmentation of Federal authority, without a diminution of State authority; at sovereignty in the Union, and complete independence in the members. They still, in fine, seem to cherish with blind devotion the political monster of an *imperium in imperio*."

"There was a time when we were told that breaches, by the States, of the regulations of the Federal authority, were not to be expected; that a sense of common interest would preside over the conduct of the respective members, and would beget a full compliance with all the constitutional requisitions of the Union. This language, at the present day, would appear as wild as a great part of what we now hear from the same quarter will be thought, when we shall have received further lessons from that best oracle of wisdom, experience. It at all

3

times betrayed an ignorance of the true springs by which human conduct is actuated, and belied the original inducements to the establishment of civil power. Why has government been instituted at all? Because the passions of men will not conform to the dictates of reason and justice, without constraint. Has it been found that bodies of men act with more rectitude and greater disinterestedness than individuals? The contrary of this has been inferred by all accurate observers of the conduct of mankind; and the inference is founded upon obvious reasons. Regard to reputation has a less active influence, when the infamy of a bad action is to be divided among a number, than when it is to fall upon a single one. A spirit of faction, which is apt to mingle its poison in the deliberations of all bodies of men, will often hurry the persons of whom they are composed, into improprieties and excesses, for which they would blush in a private capacity."

§ 4. *The radical vice of the Confederation practically continued in the Constitution.*

"The great and radical vice, in the construction of the existing Confederation, is in the principle of LEGISLATION for STATES or GOVERNMENTS in their CORPORATE or COLLECTIVE CAPACITIES, and as contradistinguished from the INDIVIDUALS of whom they consist."—*Hamilton.*

This was the inherent vice in the former theory. As already stated, the fundamental vice in our existing theory, is the attempt to divide, between the Federal and State Governments, that supreme element or principle, which we call sovereignty. These two vices, in their ultimate practical results, are much the same. They differ in degree, and in the period of time required to plainly develop their legitimate tendencies; but they are still the same in practical effect.

Under our Constitutional theory, the Federal Government is one of delegated limited powers; while the powers of the separate State Governments consist of those reserved. Both the Federal and State Governments are Governments of limited powers.

The Constitution assumes to define the line of separation between the delegated and reserved powers. But this task, in the very nature of things, is one of paramount difficulty. Conceding that the framers of the instrument had, in all cases, a clear conception of that which they intended to convey to others; still they were compelled to clothe their ideas in human language. Mr. Madison, in the thirty-seventh number of the *Federalist*, has very forcibly expressed himself in reference to the great difficulty of correct definition. He says:

"The use of words is to express ideas. Perspicuity therefore requires, not only that the ideas should be distinctly formed, but that they should be expressed by words distinctly and exclusively appropriated to them. But no language is so copious as to supply words and phrases for every complex idea, or so correct as not to include many, equivocally denoting different ideas. Hence it must happen, that however accurately objects may be discriminated in themselves, and however accurately the discrimination may be conceived, the definition of them may be rendered inaccurate by the inaccuracy of the terms in which it is delivered. And this unavoidable inaccuracy must be greater or less, according to the complexity and novelty of the objects defined. When the Almighty himself condescends to address mankind in their own language, his meaning, luminous as it must be, is rendered dim and doubtful, by the cloudy medium through which it is communicated."

And Webster, in his reply to Hayne, very justly said:

"No definition can be so clear as to avoid possibility of doubt; no limitation so precise as to exclude all uncertainty."

The Constitution is a very concise instrument, and yet within its narrow limits are contained the definitions and limitations of our complex theory of government. From its nature as a fundamental law, it could only lay down general principles in general terms. It could only deal in generals, and not in particulars.

The right to determine the extent of its own powers in the last resort,* must, of necessity, reside either in the General Gov-

---

* A distinction is often taken between the assumed right of Nullification and Secession. But it would seem that they both substantially rest upon the same basis, namely: the alleged right of each separate State to determine for itself, in the last resort, the extent of its own powers; and, by necessary consequence, the extent of the delegated powers of the Federal Government. It being true that the action of the General Government, beyond its delegated powers, is null and void; it follows, of

ernment, or in that of each separate State. This ultimate right must exist somewhere in the theory ; as there can be no peaceful and efficient means to settle controversies regarding the relative powers of the two jurisdictions. If we concede this sovereign right to exist in each State, then it is clear that the Constitution is, in substance and effect, but the Articles of the old Confederation. The only difference is, that while under the former theory, the acts of Congress had to be executed by the separate States within the limits of each ; under the Constitution, the separate States can defeat the action of the United States, by direct interposition. In one case non-action, and in the other action, will accomplish the same end. But the constitutional power of the separate States to accomplish the purpose intended is the same, the mere *mode* only being different.

If we concede, however, that it is the right of the General Government, under the Constitution, to determine the extent of its own powers in the last resort ; still the practical difficulty is not wholly, but only partially, obviated. As the Federal Government is one of limited powers, its action beyond the scope of these powers must be void. The inevitable result of a want of power in the agent, is to render the act null and void ; and,

necessity, that if the ultimate right of constitutional construction rests with each State, then the State can nullify or secede, at her election.

As the right to determine the extent of its own powers must necessarily exist in government, it has been often doubted whether limitations of power were of any ultimate practical utility. In other words, whether the power of *construction* was not practically equivalent to the power of *legislation*. The objection is good against a theory of government, which makes no provision for its own amendment. By an abuse of the power of construction, the will of the framers of the Constitution may be violated ; and, in the contemplation of such a theory of government, there is no remedy. The extreme right of revolution exists *in fact*, but not in the contemplation of the governmental theory ; as that extreme right is never sanctioned by any constitution.

But the objection as against a constitution which provides for its own amendment, is not wholly, but only partially true. The will of the framers of such a constitution may be violated for *a time ;* but as the power to amend always exists, the misconstruction can be corrected. Our courts hold the same relation to the Constitution that the courts of England now bear to the Acts of Parliament. Her judges under both theories, now hold their offices during good behavior, and the powers of the framers of our Constitution, and those of Parliament, have no theoretical limitation. On the contemplation of each theory, they can do any thing within the limits of physical possibility. The judges in England may misconstrue an Act of Parliament, but that body can amend the Act, and make it too plain to be misunderstood. So, of our Constitution, it can be made plainer, and the evils of misconstruction thus be removed.

consequently, all persons, natural and artificial, have the undoubted right to disregard the act. An unconstitutional measure of Congress is no *law*, but simply a void act.

§ 5. *The same subject continued.*

If it be true, (as we think it is,) that, in the contemplation of the existing Constitution, the Federal Government has the right to determine the extent of its own powers in the last resort; and, of consequence, the extent of the powers reserved to the separate States; then these several positions would seem to be correct:

1. If the question be executive, the right of *final* decision rests with the President.*

2. If legislative, with Congress.

3. If judicial, with the Supreme Court.

4. And the question, whether the particular matter be executive, legislative, or judicial, with the same Court.

This view makes the Constitution consistent in theory, and avoids, *theoretically*, the radical vice of the Confederation. But is the difficulty avoided *practically?* Has not our theory sanctioned the continued existence of great separate organized, and, in many respects, antagonistic communities within the Federal territorial jurisdiction? Has it not, in fact, permitted the continuance of powers inimical, in practice, to the successful and peaceful operation of the Federal Government?

For the purpose of illustration, we will suppose the question in controversy to be judicial. The President cannot act upon it at all; neither can, Congress; and the Judiciary must wait until the question is brought before it. Courts must await the action of parties. It may be years before any one may choose to bring up a case involving the point in controversy. In the mean time, the States, as well as other parties, must act upon their own construction. When, therefore, a new and difficult question involving State rights comes up, the States are prone to decide in their own favor; and having once committed

---

* "The act of Feb. 28, 1795, (1 Statutes at Large, 424,) which confers power on the President to call forth the militia in certain exigencies, is a constitutional law, and the President is the exclusive and final judge whether the exigency has arisen."—(12 Wheaton, 19.)

themselves, the pride of sovereignty and the impulses of passion, will make them adhere with obstinacy to their opinions; and although the controversy may be peacefully settled, the angry conflict between the two jurisdictions leaves its sting behind. It is also true, that individuals may have very great confidence in their own construction of the Constitution, especially where their interests, passions, or prejudices are concerned; but this pride of opinion is not so great as it is in sovereignties; and individuals have not that power which resides in States. The decisions of Courts can be more readily executed upon individuals standing alone, than upon great organizations, or upon individuals under their protection, rightful or assumed.

The following remarks of Hamilton, in the fifteenth number of the *Federalist*, though made with reference to the States while under the Confederation, are alike applicable to them under the Constitution :

" In addition to all this, there is, in the nature of sovereign power, an impatience of control, which disposes those who are invested with the exercise of it, to look with an evil eye upon all external attempts to restrain or direct its operations. From this spirit it happens, that in every political association which is formed upon the principle of uniting in one common interest a number of lesser sovereignties, there will be found a kind of eccentric tendency in the subordinate or inferior orbs, by the operation of which there will be a perpetual effort to fly from the common centre. This tendency is not difficult to be accounted for. It has its origin in the law of power. Power, controlled or abridged, is almost always the rival and enemy of that power by which it is controlled or abridged."

By our theory, the same citizen owes allegiance to two separate and distinct powers, both of which he knows are of *limited* jurisdiction ; and that the action of each beyond its constitutional sphere, is *void*. But he is not always able to know which is constitutionally right in its claims to his obedience. He is often left in doubt; and while his best judgment may tell him that his superior allegiance is due to the Federal Government, his heart is with his State, not only because she is nearest in position to him, and can first reach him by her process, but because he finds her in possession, under the Constitution itself, of all those important powers of government that must virtually

affect his dearest interests. The power over life, liberty, reputation, and property, is reserved to his State.

Our experience, short as it has been, and under the favor-
able circumstances heretofore attending our experiment, has
shown that the predictions of Hamilton,* by far the greatest
statesman of our country, were true. In almost every instance
when a controversy has arisen between the Federal Government
and that of a State, the latter carried its point. Even the case

* "It is a known fact in human nature that its affections are commonly weak
in proportion to the distance or diffusiveness of the object. Upon the principle that a
man is more attached to his family than to his neighborhood, to his neighborhood than
to the community at large, the people of each State would be apt to feel a stronger bias
towards their local Governments, than towards the Government of the Union, unless
the force of that principle should be destroyed by a much better administration of the
latter."

"There is one transcendent advantage belonging to the province of State Governments which alone suffices to place the matter in a clear and satisfactory light. I mean
the ordinary administration of civil and criminal justice. This, of all others, is the
most powerful, most universal, and most attractive source of popular obedience and
attachment. It is this which, being the immediate and visible guardian of life and
property, having its benefits and its terrors in constant activity before the public eye,
regulating all those personal interests, and familiar concerns, to which the sensibility
of individuals is more immediately awake—contributes more than any other circum-
stance, to impress upon the minds of the people affection, esteem, and reverence towards
the Government. This great cement of society, which will diffuse itself almost wholly
through the channels of the particular Governments, independent of all other causes of
influence, would insure them so decided an empire over their respective citizens, as to
render them at all times a complete counterpoise, and not unfrequently dangerous rivals
to the power of the Union."

"Though the ancient feudal systems were not, strictly speaking, confederacies, yet
they partook of the nature of that species of association. There was a common head,
chieftain, or sovereign, whose authority extended over the whole nation, and a number
of subordinate vassals, or feudatories, who had large portions of land allotted to them,
and numerous trains of *inferior* vassals or retainers, who occupied and cultivated that
land upon the tenure of fealty, or obedience to the persons of whom they held it. Each
principal vassal was a kind of sovereign within his particular demesnes. The consequences of this situation were a continual opposition to the authority of the sovereign,
and frequent wars between the great barons, or chief feudatories themselves. The
power of the head of the nation was commonly too weak, either to preserve the public
peace, or to protect the people against the oppression of their immediate lords. This
period of European affairs is emphatically styled by historians the times of feudal an-
archy."—(*Federalist*, No. 17.)

"Reasons have been already given to induce a supposition that the State Governments will too naturally be prone to a rivalship with that of the Union, the foundation
of which will be the love of power; and that, in any contest between the federal head
and one of its members, the people will be most apt to unite with their local government."—(Id., No. 25.)

of South Carolina in 1833, in reference to the question of the tariff, did not constitute an entire exception, as is too often supposed. It is true that President Jackson promptly issued his proclamation, in which he assumed decisive ground in support of the laws of the nation; but it is equally true that the tariff was so modified as to receive the support of the representation of that State in Congress. In other words, it was a *compromise* which *decided* nothing.

But in the contest between the Federal Judiciary and the State of Georgia in 1831, in reference to the rights of the Cherokee Indians under a treaty of the United States, that State carried her point with a high hand, though General Jackson was then President. The following extracts from Benton's Thirty Years' View, will give some general idea of its character:

" Judge Clayton, in whose circuit the Indian counties fell, at his first charge to the grand jury assured the Indians of protection, warned the intermeddlers of the mischief they were doing, and of the inutility of applying to the Supreme Court . . . . . . With respect to the Supreme Court, the judge declared that he should pay no attention to its mandate—holding no writ of error to lie from the Supreme Court of the United States to his State Court—but would execute the sentence of the law, whatever it might be, in defiance of the Supreme Court; and such was the fact. Instigated by foreign interference, and relying upon its protection, one George Tassels, of Indian descent, committed a homicide in resisting the laws of Georgia—was tried for murder—convicted—condemned—and sentenced to be hanged upon a given day. A writ of error, to bring the case before itself, was obtained from the Supreme Court of the United States. . . . . . The day for the execution of Tassels came round: he was hanged: and the writ of the Supreme Court was no more heard of."—(Vol. i., 165, 166.)

The Supreme Court might have sustained the validity of the act of the Legislature of Georgia extending her jurisdiction over the Cherokees, had the case gone up to that Court; but the State Court and the Governor decided for themselves, (and fully carried out their decision,) that the Supreme Court had no jurisdiction in such cases. This was deciding the very question that was first in issue. This action of the State authorities was based upon one of two grounds: 1. That the right to determine, in the last resort, the extent of its own powers, rests with each State; or, 2. That the Constitution has provided no mode of determining the question of conflicting jurisdiction between the Federal and State tribunals, but has left them in perpetual conflict. Col. Benton denies the alleged right of Nullification and Secession, while he inconsistently sustains the action of Georgia.

§ 6. *The same subject further considered.*

The mode in which the Constitution was ratified, has given rise to great doubts, as to the true character of the Government created by the instrument. The historical fact is certain, that the States existed, as distinct sovereignties, at the time that instrument was formed; and that each State ratified the Constitution for itself alone, acting in its organized capacity as a unit. The little State of Delaware, for example, would not have been bound by the Constitution, without her own separate ratification, though every other State had done so.

Though it be not within the scope of this work to enter into any elaborate discussion of a question which has so much divided the public men of the nation; yet the writer may be permitted to state concisely his view of a single point.

As the States existed when the Constitution was formed, there was but one of two logical modes in which this could

* "And the writ of the Supreme Court was *no more heard of*," says Col. Benton. This is a melancholy truth. Here was a court claiming to be the supreme judicial tribunal of a great nation, that could not even execute its process. Who can have any confidence in, or respect for, a court of such extravagant pretensions; but, in fact, possessing so little *real* power? True, the individual, in whose person a great and decisive principle of law and justice was violated, was obscure, and of mixed blood. Still, for that very reason, the justice and majesty of the law should have been vindicated. It is the glory of a true theory of government, that its protection is alike over all, and equally imparted and efficient in all cases. History shows that the great and eternal principles of justice are always *first* violated in the person of some poor and obscure individual. But the principle itself, once violated with impunity, ceases to command respect.

The remarks of the profound De Tocqueville, (275, note,) that "the governments of the States are in reality the authorities which direct society in America," is unfortunately too true. The result has necessarily been to form sectional and antagonistic parties in our country.

have been done. The first, by the separate action of the States as already organized communities; and the second, by the States first dissolving themselves into their original elements, and thus permitting the people, acting as one mass, to form their own Constitution. The first method was the proper one, under the existing circumstances; for the reason, that so long as a people remain organized, they must act through their organization. It was the most simple, concise, and direct mode of action, and equally efficient; for it must be conceded, that, though the Constitution was formed by the separate action of each State, they had still the clear right, *in this very mode*, to confer upon the Government any powers they pleased. If they had the right to delegate a part, they had equally the right to delegate the whole of their own powers. Therefore, the *mere mode* in which the Constitution was formed is not *conclusive*, but only *prima facie* evidence of its true character. Had the States intended to delegate *all their* powers to the Union, they could have well formed the Constitution in the manner they did adopt. At the same time, it must be admitted that the mode adopted would require the language of delegation to be more explicit and clear; because the *prima facie* presumption would always be, that the States did not mean to delegate their powers, and thus cripple or annihilate themselves. Governments, at least in theory, are intended to be perpetual; and the law will not, therefore, admit any abridgment of their existing powers, or their entire annihilation, without clear proof. The language of the Constitution, though clear to a reasonable extent, is yet susceptible of being made much more explicit.

It is true, that while no theory of government can be formed, so as entirely to escape forcible resistance at all times; yet a constitution may be made so clear, as greatly to diminish the *plausible* pretences for alleged constitutional resistance; and thus force rebellious spirits to *plainly* base their action upon the true ground. The people will hesitate much longer in joining, even for the same alleged cause, a plain rebellion, than they will in vindicating, by force of arms, a plausible construction of the Constitution. The want of a more clear and explicit statement, in the Constitution, of the right of the General Government to determine its own powers, and those of the States, in the last resort, has, for *practical* purposes, continued the radical vice of the old Confederation.

§ 7. *Other effects of divided sovereignty.*

A citizen of the United States and of a State, may be twice tried, convicted, and punished for the same act. This results from the principle, that he owes allegiance to two sovereigns. It has been so repeatedly held by the Supreme Court of the United States. In the case of Moore *v.* The State of Illinois, (14 Howard, 13,) Mr. Justice Grier, in delivering the opinion of the Court, among other things, said :

" Every citizen of the United States is also a citizen of a State or Territory. He may be said to owe allegiance to two sovereigns, and may be liable to punishment for an infraction of the laws of either. The same act may be an offence or transgression of the laws of both. . . . . That either or both may (if they see fit) punish such an offender, cannot be doubted. . . . . He could not plead the punishment by one in bar to a conviction by the other ; consequently, this Court has decided, in the case of Fox *v.* The State of Ohio, (5 How. 432,) that a State may punish the offence of uttering or passing false coin, as a cheat or fraud practiced on its citizens ; and, in the case of the United States *v.* Marigold, (9 How. 560,) that Congress, in the proper exercise of its authority, may punish the same act as an offence against the United States."

Mr. Justice McLean dissented, and justly censured the principle that an individual could be punished twice for the same act ; yet he was unable to satisfy the other judges that the opinion of the Court was not truly the law. The province of a Court, even that of the Supreme Court of the United States, is simply to *declare*, not to make the law. The question whether the principle involved be just or unjust is a matter for the lawmaker, not the law-exponent, to determine. It is true, that in reference to a mere question of construction, where the language of the law is not clear, we may properly inquire into the legitimate result of a proposed interpretation. But when the meaning is plain, the courts must carry out the intention of the legislative power, though the principle, in the opinion of the Court, may be unjust ; otherwise, there could be no separation of the legislative and judicial functions.

By the second section of the third article it is provided, that the "judicial power shall extend to controversies between two or more States;" but the Constitution provides no means of enforcing the judgment of the court when rendered. In case of resistance, it might be very difficult to carry out the decision of the court. Though, from the dignity of the parties, it might be inferred, that the unsuccessful State would submit with a good grace; yet history shows that bodies of men, when exasperated, are prone to great excesses. Should the present theory continue a few years longer, some case will most probably arise that will conclusively test this question.

§ 8. *Character of the reserved powers.*

As before stated, the powers of the General Government are those *delegated*, while the powers of the States are those *reserved*. This is clearly stated in the tenth amended article:

"The powers not delegated to the United States by the Constitution, nor prohibited by it to the States, are reserved to the States respectively, as to the people."

This language is very explicit. If the power be not delegated and not prohibited, then it is reserved; but if it be either delegated or prohibited, it is not reserved. There are certain powers not delegated to the United States, that are prohibited to the States; such as, for example, the power to grant titles of nobility. Such powers belong to neither the one theory nor the other, but are prohibited to both. To ascertain the powers reserved to the States, it is necessary *first* to know the powers delegated and prohibited. *All other* powers of government, after subtracting these, are reserved to the States.

The Supreme Court of the United States has always held that the amendments to the Constitution of the United States were simply restrictions upon the powers of the General Government, and not upon those of the several States. Thus in the case of Barrow *v.* The City of Baltimore, (7 Peters, 243,) Chief Justice Marshall, in delivering the opinion of the Court, said:

"The people of the United States framed such a government for the United States as they supposed best adapted to their situation, and best calculated to promote their interests. The powers they conferred on this Government were to be exercised by itself; and the limitations on power, if expressed in general terms, are naturally, and, we think, necessarily applicable to the government created by the instrument. They are limitations of power granted in the instrument itself; not of distinct governments framed by different persons and for different purposes. . . . . But it is universally understood, it is part of the history of the day, that the great Revolution which established the Constitution of the United States was not effected without immense opposition. . . . . In almost every convention by which the Constitution was adopted, amendments to guard against the abuse of power were recommended. These amendments demanded security against the apprehended encroachments of the General Government, not against those of the local governments." *

Hence, in that case, the Court determined that the provision of the Constitution, that private property should not be taken for public use without just compensation, did not apply to the States. The same principle was again held by that Court in the case of Withers v. Brickley, (20 Howard, 84.) In the case of Satterlee v. Matthewson, (2 Peters, 380,) it was decided that there was nothing in the Constitution of the United States which forbid the Legislature of a State from exercising judicial functions.

In the case of the Bank of the State of Alabama v. Dalton, (9 Howard, 530,) it appeared that the plaintiff recovered judgment against the defendant in the State of Alabama, February 7, 1843, and afterwards sued the defendant upon the record of

---

* In the thirty-eighth number of the *Federalist*, Mr. Madison enumerates the principal objections urged against the Constitution ; and from that it will be seen how few persons objected to the weakness of the Federal Government. The current of ideas ran strongly in favor of the States, and against the alleged danger of a strong central government. It may seem remarkable that so few minds perceived the defects that time has shown to exist. This, however, was the case with respect to the radical vice of the Confederation, speaking of which, in the same number, Mr. Madison says :

" It is observable that among the numerous objections and amendments suggested by the several States, when those articles were submitted for their ratification, not one is found which alludes to the great and radical error, which on actual trial has discovered itself."

The influence which the small States exerted in the formation of the Constitution, and their jealousy of the powers of the Federal Government, are shown by the proceedings of the Convention, and may be seen in the fifth article, where it is provided that amendments ratified by three-fourths of the States shall be valid ; provided, that " no State, without its consent, shall be deprived of its equal suffrage in the Senate."

this judgment, in the District Court of the United States for the Northern District of the State of Mississippi, November 10, 1846. Defendant pleaded the Statute of Limitations of the State of Mississippi, passed in 1844, " which (1) bars all suits on judgments recovered within the State after the lapse of seven years ; and (2) all suits on judgments obtained out of the State in six years, in cases of judgments thereafter rendered ; and (3) all suits on judgments obtained out of the State before the act was passed are barred, unless suit be brought thereon within two years next after the date of the act. On this latter provision the defence depends." Mr. Justice Catron, who delivered the opinion of the Court, remarked :

" The stringency of the case is, that the Act of Limitations of Mississippi invites to the State and protects absconding debtors from other States, by refusing a creditor a remedy on his judgment, which is in full force in the State whence the debtor absconded. . . . . In administering justice to enforce contracts and judgments, the States of the Union act independently of each other, and their courts are governed by the laws and municipal regulations of that State where a remedy is sought, unless they are controlled by the Constitution of the United States, or by laws enacted under its authority."

The Court, in that case, decided, that " the State law is not opposed to the Constitution of the United States, or to the act of Congress of 1790." The same decision was made in a case reported in 18 Howard, 249.

This act not only made an invidious distinction between judgments rendered in and out of the State, but it allowed a very short time in which to bring suits upon the latter class of judgments. As the State had the power to fix the period of two years, it is difficult to set any limits to that power, and a much shorter period of time might have been designated. By this iniquitous measure, the fraudulent debtor was *legally* enabled to pay his creditor by running off. By the act, absconding to avoid honest debts was made a virtue.

§ 9. *The same subject continued.*

In the case of Mager *v.* Grima, (8 Howard, 490,) it appeared that John Mager, a citizen of the State of Louisiana, left a legacy to his sister, a resident of France. The statute of Louisiana imposed a tax of ten per cent. upon legacies to foreigners not domiciled within the State.* Chief Justice Taney, in delivering the opinion of the Court, said:

"Now the law in question is nothing more than the exercise of the power which every State and sovereignty possesses of regulating the manner and the term upon which property, real and personal, within its dominion may be transmitted by last will and testament, or by inheritance; and of prescribing who shall and who shall not be capable of taking it."

The State had the power to impose the tax, and fix the rate; and it would seem that the discrimination made against foreigners might have been extended to the citizens of other States, and of any particular State. So, the general power "of prescribing who shall and who shall not take property by last will and testament, or by inheritance," would extend to the citizens of other States, and of any particular State.

"A writ of error from the Supreme Court of the United States to the Supreme Court of a State, directs the latter court to transmit the record of the case to the upper court." (Chief Justice Taney. Scott v. Sandford, 19 Howard, 453.)

But how the Supreme Court could compel a compliance with its writ, in case of refusal by the State Court, is a very difficult case to determine. In the report of the case of Hunter v. Martin, (4 Munford's Vir. Rep., 1,) it is stated that "the appellee Martin obtained a writ of error from the Supreme Court of the United States, requiring the Court of Appeals of Virginia to certify the record for re-examination by that court. The Honorable William Fleming, president of this Court, complied with the writ by certifying a transcript '*improvidently*,' as was afterwards decided by himself as well as the other judges."

In that case it was held by the Supreme Court of the United States, that "the return of a copy of the record, under the seal of the court, certified by the clerk, and annexed to the writ of error, is a sufficient return in such a case." Head note of the case. (6 Wheaton, 304.) In the case of Ableman v. Booth,

* To constitute domicile, "there must be actual residence in the place, with the intention that it is to be a principal and permanent residence." Language of Mr. Justice Wayne in delivering the opinion of the Court, in the case of Ennis v. Smith, (14 Howard, 423.)

(21 Howard, 506,) it appeared that the Supreme Court of Wisconsin directed the clerk of that court to " make no return to the writ of error, and to enter no order upon the journals or records of the court concerning the same." The Supreme Court of the United States, under the circumstances, permitted Mr. Black, the attorney-general of the United States, to file a certified copy of the record, which had been *previously* obtained. The Court was thus enabled to proceed with the case; but had the statute of the State made it a criminal act in the clerk to certify a copy of the record for any purpose, or had that officer refused to make out the transcript, the question of the power of the Supreme Court of the United States to compel a compliance with the writ of error, would have been brought up for decision. According to newspaper report, that Court has lately decided, upon the application of the Governor of Kentucky for a writ of mandamus to compel the Governor of Ohio to surrender a fugitive from justice, that the Federal tribunals have no power over State officers. But until a full and authentic report of the case is made, we may not understand correctly the exact ground assumed by the Court. In the case of Tassels, already referred to, the prisoner was executed in defiance of the writ of error; and there seems to have been no power in the Supreme Court of the United States to vindicate its authority, by punishing the offending judge of the State Court.

§ 10. *The same subject further considered.*

By the second section of the first article of the Constitution, members of Congress shall be chosen every second year by the people of the several States, and " the electors in each State shall have the qualifications requisite for electors of the most numerous branch of the State Legislature." It therefore belongs to each State to determine who shall and who shall not be citizens of that State. The power of naturalization is exclusively conferred upon Congress; and the exercise of this power only makes the alien a citizen of the United States, and not a citizen of any particular State.*

---

* The question whether a person of African descent can become a citizen of the United States, was not determined in the case of Scott *v.* Sandford, only three justices deciding that he *could not*, namely: Taney, Wayne, and Daniels. Justices Grier, Nel-

"Every State," says Chief Justice Taney, "has the undoubted right to determine the status or domestic and social condition of the persons domiciled within its territory, except in so far as the powers of the States in this respect are restrained, as duties and obligations imposed upon them by the Constitution of the United States."—(10 Howard, 93.)

And Mr. Justice Curtis, in his most able opinion, delivered in the case of Scott v. Sandford, (19 Howard,) uses this language:

"To what citizens the elective franchise shall be confided, is a question to be determined by each State, in accordance with its own views of the necessities or expediences of its own condition. What civil rights shall be enjoyed by its citizens, and whether all shall enjoy the same, or how they may be gained or lost, are to be determined in the same way."

The clause of the Constitution which restrains the powers of the several States, and imposes duties upon them in reference to citizens of other States, is found in the second section of the third article, in these words:

"The citizens of each State shall be entitled to all privileges and immunities of citizens in the several States."

This clause is obscure; but from the opinion of Chief Justice Taney, in the case of Scott v. Sandford, (19 Howard, 416,) the following conclusions may be drawn:

son, Campbell, and Catron concurred in the *judgment* of the court upon *other* grounds, and expressed no opinion upon *this* point. Justices McLean and Curtis dissented. It was conceded by all the justices, that each State could make any person a citizen of the State. There was no difference of opinion between Chief Justice Taney and Mr. Justice Curtis in reference to the naturalization of *foreigners*. But as to *natives*, there was this difference: Chief Justice Taney, while clearly conceding the right of each State to make any one—native or foreign born—a citizen of the State, denied the right of the State to make even a *native* of African descent, a citizen of the *United States*. Mr. Justice Curtis, on the contrary, said:

"And my opinion is, that, under the Constitution of the United States, every person born on the soil of a State, who is a citizen of that State, by force of its Constitution and laws, is also a citizen of the United States."

This language is very clear and explicit; and *this* position was sustained by Mr. Justice Curtis, by a force of reasoning and authority that would seem to be unanswerable. But as the Constitution *only* gives Congress power in reference to *naturalization*, and confers no power as to *natives;* it is clear, that if the proposition of Mr. Justice Curtis be correct, the converse of it must be equally true, namely: that each State may *exclude* any *native* of the State—white or colored—from citizenship, both of the particular State, and of the United States.

1. It exempts persons who are at the same time both citizens of the United States and of a State, and being in another State, from any special laws and police regulations not applicable to citizens of the latter State.

2. It gives them the right to enter any other State, singly or in companies, without pass or passport, and without obstruction, to sojourn there so long as they please, and go when and where they please, unless they transgress some law applicable to citizens of the State.

3. It gives them the full liberty of speech in public and private, so far as enjoyed by the citizens of the State.

4. It gives them the right to hold public meetings, to keep and carry arms, so far as citizens of the State would be permitted to do so.

It will be seen that none of these privileges, secured by the Constitution of the United States, relate at all to *State citizenship;* but that the complete power over that right is reserved to each State respectively. For example, the State of California, by a provision of her Constitution, could exclude all persons born within any particular State or States from ever becoming citizens of California.

Any one who will examine the subject carefully, will readily find that the mass of powers reserved to the States are not only the most important powers of Government, but that they are unlimited by the Constitution of the United States. And if we follow the rule of construction laid down by the Supreme Court of the United States, (and followed by most of the State Courts, if not by all,) that the limitations of power contained in the amendments to the Constitution of the United States, apply *only* to the Government created by the instrument itself; then it is clear that the States possess such a mass of powers, that they can, by a simple abuse of those powers, render the Union ultimately intolerable. For example, the power of one State to harass another by hostile legislation and insulting resolutions, is entirely without any efficient and peaceful remedy. The most partial and invidious legislation may be resorted to, and the most harsh and insulting resolution passed by the Legislatures of the different States. Any State may establish a religion, or prohibit the free exercise thereof, abridge the freedom of the press or of speech, take private property for public uses

without just compensation, deny the right of petition and the
right to bear arms. It will be seen that the limitations contained in the first amendment relate expressly to Congress, and
not to the States.

It is very true that this mass of despotic power reserved to
the States, is, *at present*, restrained by the provisions of the
State Constitutions; but the power to amend exists in each
State; and by amendment these restrictions could be removed.
And we have, especially of late, seen enough of sectional bitterness and State hostility, to give us most reasonable apprehension for the future.

§ 11. *The general corruption of our public men.*

The general corruption of our public men is properly at-
tributable to the infamous principle, that " to the victors belong
the spoils." Under the withering influence of this most vicious
maxim, our elections, State and National, have practically become contests, more for the spoils of office, than for the success
of great principles; unless, indeed, it be those *seven* principles
mentioned by John Randolph of Roanoke: "*five loaves and
two fishes.*" And this mercenary struggle is not only for those
offices necessary for the due and proper administration of public
justice, but for mere nominal positions, created by unscrupulous
partisans to reward their friends. To what extent the true principles of government, and the rights of our entire nation, as well
as of justice, are often sacrificed by those in power, upon the
altar of private friendship and of false pity, is shown by a statement of Col. Benton:

" He [Mr. Jefferson] told me himself, not long before his
death, (Christmas, 1824,) . . . . . that he had failed to remove
many who deserved it, but who were spared through the inter-
cession of friends and concern for their distressed families."—
(Thirty Years' View, 162.)

This fact does not add to the reputation of Mr. Jefferson as
a statesman. The same weakness that would keep an unfit
person in office, would lead to the creation of an office for his
benefit. Mr. Hallam justly remarks, in substance, in his Constitutional History, that weak princes are generally under the
control of their domestics. The want of a proper conception of

duty, and the failure to truly discern the best ultimate humanity, will very naturally lead to the sacrifice of principle to feeling, and the rights and interests of the great and mighty future, to the pressing but trifling expediency of the moment.

The really great Washington had a right conception of the duties of his position, was too just to sacrifice duty to feeling, and rose above those temptations which lesser minds could not withstand. In one of his letters, he says :

" My friend I receive with cordial welcome. He is welcome to my house, and welcome to my heart ; but with all his good qualities, he is not a man of business. His opponent, with all his politics so hostile to me, *is* a man of business. My private feelings have nothing to do in the case. I am not George Washington, but President of the United States. As George Washington, I would do this man any kindness in my power—as President of the United States I can do nothing."

How forcible and just is that sentence : " I am not George Washington, but President of the United States." In his individual capacity he had the right to do any thing he could for his friend, but in his capacity as President he had no right to prostitute his official powers to gratify his mere personal feelings, or to discharge mere personal obligations. He was the officer of the Nation, and not the individual, George Washington.

But the prostituting and undermining principle, that " to the victors belong the spoils," is itself but a *secondary* cause, and but the legitimate result of other causes found in the theory of our Government. The defects in our theory which give rise to this vicious maxim, are the short duration of the terms of office, and the re-eligibility of incumbents.

Evils which arise from defective theories of government, do not generally manifest themselves in their full force at once. They generally require time for their full maturity ; and the length of time required depends upon circumstances. If we examine the history of our Government, we shall find that the spoils principle was but *gradually* introduced ; a very strong proof that it has its origin in our theory itself.

At the time Washington was elected, parties had not been fully organized. Though the seeds of party division had been sown in the National Convention, and in the different State

Conventions, they had not had time to mature during the administration of Washington. Besides this, his popularity was too decisive to admit of any successful competition. But when he had retired to private life, and his successor, the elder Adams, had taken his position, party lines were strictly drawn.

Mr. Adams agreed in his views with Washington, and made no removals from office upon purely political grounds, there being but nine removals during his term of four years. He was a candidate for re-election, but was defeated by Mr. Jefferson; and there is reason to believe that his feelings were wounded because he was not permitted to serve for two terms, according to the precedent set by Washington. The contest between the friends of the two was very bitter; and under the influence of these circumstances, Mr. Adams made some appointments, at the close of his term, which had the appearance of being partisan. In reference to which, Mr. Jefferson, in his letter to Elbridge Gerry, says:

"Mr. Adams's last appointments, when he knew he was appointing counsellors and aids for me, not for himself, I set aside as fast as depends on me."

§ 12. *The same subject continued.*

The election of Mr. Jefferson, it must be conceded, was substantially a revolution of parties; and he, therefore, found but few of his political friends in office.* The subject of removals gave him much trouble. In a letter to Mr. Lincoln, his Attorney-general, and written during the first year of his administration, among other things, he says:

"I still think our original idea as to office is best; that is,

---

* There can be no reasonable doubt of the fact that the views of Washington, Hamilton, and the elder Adams, were substantially the same in reference to political questions. Hamilton was a great favorite with Washington, having been one of his aids during the war, and Washington always had the utmost confidence in his judgment. The political education of Washington was defective. He had never regularly and thoroughly studied the science of government. But Hamilton had; and he was, therefore, a thorough statesman. At the age of thirty he was a member of the Convention, and he exhibited more true capacity than any other member, if not more than all combined. He was the only delegate who signed the Constitution for the State of New York; while eight delegates signed for Pennsylvania, and four for New Jersey. Washington showed his superior natural capacity by his due appreciation of Hamilton.

to depend, for obtaining a just participation, on deaths, resignations, and delinquencies. This will least affect the tranquillity of the people, and prevent their giving in to the suggestion
of our enemies, that ours has been a contest for office, and not
for principles. This is rather a slow operation, but it is sure,
if we pursue it steadily, which, however, has not been done
with the undeviating resolution I could have wished. To these
means of obtaining a just share in the transaction of public
business, shall be added one more, to wit, removal for electioneering activity, or open and industrious opposition to the principles of the present Government, legislative and executive.
Every officer of the Government may vote at elections according
to his conscience; but we should betray the cause committed
to our care, were we to permit the influence of official patron-
age to be used to overthrow that cause."

In reply to the remonstrance of the merchants of New
Haven, against the removal of Mr. Goodrich, collector, he
says :

"When it is considered that, during the late administration,
those who were not of a political set were excluded from all
office; when, by a steady pursuit of this measure, nearly the
whole offices of the United States were monopolized by that
set ; when the public sentiment at length declared itself, and
burst open the doors of honor and confidence to those whose
opinions they approved, was it to be imagined that this monop-
oly of office was to be continued in the hands of the minority ?
Does it violate *their equal rights* to assert the same rights also in
the majority ?   Is it *political intolerance* to claim a *proportion-
ate* share in the direction of public affairs ?   If a due *participation* of office is a matter of right, how are vacancies to be obtained ?   Those by deaths are few, by resignations none.   Can
any other mode than that by removals be proposed ? "

In the same letter, he says the total exclusion of his friends
from office " calls for prompter corrections.   I shall correct the
procedure, but that done, return *with joy* to that state of things
when the *only* question concerning a candidate shall be, is he
honest ?   Is he capable ?   Is he faithful to the Constitution ? "

Mr. Jefferson seems to have acted upon the rules laid down
by him; for during his entire administration of eight years,
there were only forty-two removals.   His three successors only

made sixteen removals : Madison five, Monroe nine, and John Quincy Adams two. During the terms of Mr. Monroe, party lines became confined and almost obliterated. It was called "the era of good feeling."

In 1816, General Jackson, in his correspondence with Mr. Monroe, said :

"Every thing depends on the selection of your ministry. In every selection, party and party feeling should be avoided. Now is the time to exterminate the *monster* called party spirit. By selecting characters most conspicuous for their probity, virtue, capacity, and firmness, *without any regard to party*, you will go far to, if not entirely, eradicate those feelings, which, on a former occasion, threw so many obstacles in the way of Government ; and perhaps have the pleasure and honor of uniting a people heretofore politically divided. *The Chief Magistrate of a great and powerful nation should never indulge in party feeling.* His conduct should be liberal and disinterested, always bearing in mind that he acts for the whole and not a part of the community. By this course you will exalt the national character, and acquire for yourself a name as imperishable as monumental marble."

But time brings about strange events ; and General Jackson himself afterwards became President, and thus had an opportunity, in his own person, to carry out the principles he had laid down some years before. He, however, found himself constrained by circumstances to depart from the path recommended to his friend, Mr. Monroe. According to the estimate of Col. Benton, as given in the first volume of his Thirty Years' View, the number of removals from office, during the eight years of President Jackson's administration, was about six hundred and ninety ; leaving still a majority of political opponents in office. Others make the number of removals much greater. But while it may be true, that a majority left in office by him were opposed to his administration, yet it must be conceded that removals were generally made in the more important and influential offices. If we compare the importance of the offices filled by his friends, with the importance of those filled by his opponents, the preponderance was greatly in favor of his administration.

The spoils principle was sedulously cultivated under the

administration of Mr. Van Buren, and has now become the fixed law of party. We all remember the sad fate of General Harrison. The old soldier sought shelter under the roof of the late Judge Woodbury. "In God's name," said he, "a night of peace and quietness—I am dying for rest. The office-seekers are killing me." In a few days he was dead. Whether the same cause had any share in producing the death of General Taylor it is difficult to determine.

§ 13. *The same subject further considered.*

In the progress of human affairs, great and complex questions must, in the very nature of things, arise, from time to time, under every government, whatever may be its form. In a despotism, these questions will be determined by the person at the head of the government, with the aid of his ministers; but in a representative government, these questions must be decided by persons chosen by the people. For this reason, all great questions of governmental principle or policy, (except in special cases,) must be discussed before the voters, and must lead to party divisions among the people themselves, followed by all the evils flowing from party spirit, unless checked or diminished by some compensating power.

The entire executive power of the Federal Government is vested in the office of President. In the very nature of executive power, it must be a unit. For this reason, the power of removal from subordinate executive offices must be placed in the President. To require a formal trial in each particular case, accompanied with its doubtful result and long delays, would so cripple the executive power as to render it inefficient, and its operation unsteady. There must be many cases, perhaps a majority, where the necessity of removal may be palpable to the President; but, from the strict proof required in formal trials, and the artful efforts of the subordinate to conceal his fault under plausible pretences, it might be very difficult to procure a conviction. And to give the President the power of removal, and then clog it with vexatious and impracticable restrictions, would nullify the power given. There must be force, unity, and energy in the Executive; and to secure these, he must be left with means commensurate with the great ends intended by the creation of the office.

The office of President being elective, and for a very *short* term, *frequent* revolutions of parties must follow. When a President of a different party comes into office, and finds, as he will certainly do, the offices filled by those whose political views differ from his own, and who will very naturally be averse to aid him in carrying out his measures, what is he to do ? He is about to introduce new measures of principle or policy, and can he safely trust the result of the experiment to unfriendly hands? Would it be wise to do so ? It would not. What, then, can he do, but make removals upon mere political grounds ? And when he does make removals upon such grounds, he acts upon a principle that inevitably leads, sooner or later, to the practical adoption of the maxim, that " to the victors belong the spoils."

We see the truth of this exemplified under the administration of Mr. Jefferson. He assumed that it was the *right* of both parties to have a due share in the administration of public affairs ; and, to give this right effect, in *his case*, it was necessary to create vacancies by removals for mere political reasons. But this right once conceded, it became, in due time, evident, that when one party under one administration, enjoyed *all* the offices, the other, on coming into power, had the right to *all*, to place the two upon an equality. The main principle of Mr. Jefferson necessarily leads to this result.

In his letter to Mr. Lincoln, he proposed removals only for two causes : official delinquency, and active partisanship. But in case officers did their duty, and were not active partisans, how could the necessary number of vacancies be had, in order to give to each party its due share of the offices ? " Those by deaths were few, by resignations none." It was also found out, in the course of time, that the subordinate was placed in this predicament, namely : if he refused to exert himself actively for those in power, he was dismissed ; and if he did, he incurred the certainty of dismissal, if the opposite party should be successful. He, therefore, would most naturally take that course which would escape the certain and immediate danger, and risk that which was uncertain and remote. Under Mr. Jefferson's rule, if one President should require his subordinates to take an active part in elections, his successful competitor would be bound to remove all who had done so. Though Mr. Jefferson attempted to put limitations to his rule, yet it was based upon the principle of removal for mere political reasons ; and he was, in fact, the first President to act substantially upon the same rule, which has since very naturally become general.

It being true, that parties must exist under every form of representative government, aspirants for office will necessarily divide themselves between the different parties : some from principle, most from love of office. To succeed, parties must be organized ; and organization requires some one organ through which the party can speak. Hence conventions have become the resort of all parties. In these conventions, aspirants are all required to pledge themselves, in advance, to support the nominees.

This pledge gives the action of the convention very great force with the party, no matter by what means the nominations may have been brought about. The favorites of the party may have been defeated by unfair means, but still there is no practical remedy. To abandon the nominations, is to insure defeat. The offices being numerous, and the terms very short, the number of aspirants for present nomination, and of expectants for the future, must necessarily be very great. Each aspirant and expectant has his particular friends, and those again their own ; and putting all these together, they form a combination too powerful to be successfully resisted. The defeated aspirants could not, with any sort of consistency, themselves become candidates before the people, after having pledged themselves to support the nominees. Independent candidates may be brought out, professing to be of the same party ; but their motives and principles are subject to great doubt. The nominees and all their friends will accuse the independent candidates of factious opposition, and of a secret desire to defeat the great principles for which the party contends. These self-nominated candidates, as they are called, cannot hope to obtain votes from the members of the opposite party ; and even those of their own party who are not aspirants or expectants, and who sincerely object to the nominees, and abhor the nefarious manner in which the nominations were made, are reduced to the alternative of voting for the nominees, or seeing the defeat of their own party principles. As a choice of evils, they generally, *at last*, vote the ticket. The result is the defeat of the independent candidates. In time, aspirants and expectants learn to become very cautious of opposition to nominations.

§ 14. *The same subject further considered.*

Experience having shown the force of nominations when made, (a nomination being often equivalent to an election,) the greatest efforts of aspirants will be directed to that end. Those who are unscrupulous will, of course, not hesitate to make any promises or combinations deemed necessary to attain success. These promises and combinations can be so adroitly made, that they cannot, at the time, be easily detected. Aspirants of strict integrity and true delicacy, will hesitate to come in competition with the unscrupulous, because they consider themselves as placed in a position where they not only have not an equal chance of success, but where they must, if defeated, suffer the mortification of having been overcome by an unworthy competitor, and by unfair means.

For example, we will suppose an aspirant for the Presidency, permits his name to go before a national convention. He finds it filled with many who are themselves aspirants for office; and most of those members who are not, have particular friends who are. *He* is *now* dependent upon them for a nomination; but when elected, they or their friends will, in turn, be dependent upon him for appointments. If they give him *their* support, it is with the expectation that their services will not be overlooked. But whether any expectation be indulged or not as to *particular* individuals, all aspirants for office under the new President, will unite in insisting that all political opponents shall be removed, and political friends appointed. The success of the party, they say, requires it. Justice to those who have borne the heat and burden of the day requires it. The other party has done it, so must we. It is the law of party. No party can now succeed without it.

And when the new President comes into office, he finds himself overwhelmed with applications for appointments; and though the condition of the nation be ever so perilous, requiring the most prompt and decisive action, he must still consume several weeks of precious time in filling offices with partisan friends; because he knows the insatiate applicants, like the importunate woman mentioned in Scripture, may, by their continual coming, weary him. The only way to get an opportunity to attend to the most pressing wants of the nation, is *first* to attend to the wishes of individuals.

The short term of the office of President, and the re-eligibility of the incumbent, keep party spirit always in existence, ever active and vigorous, and hosts of aspirants always in the field, hungry, hopeful, and clamorous for office. When a new President comes into office, he finds himself committed by a thousand pledges, (often contradictory,) and party expectations innumerable, and generally unreasonable. His time and strength are consumed in vain and useless discussions; and his views are trammelled, and his official action hampered by his party connections. In *form*, he is a ruler; but in fact, he is the slave of office-seekers. The same circumstances that affect him, affect his cabinet and members of Congress. They have no time to become statesmen; because their time and intellects are mainly exhausted in studying and making political combinations, and in laying out plans for the gratification of their ambition or revenge. This is the reason why, of late years especially, our public men generally have such warm friends and bitter enemies. The first are attached by personal obligations, while the second are impelled by personal hate. We see the effect upon the members of nearly every department of the Government. The House of Representatives has very little dignity, the Senate has much degenerated of late, and the office of President itself has not escaped.

And when we go from the Federal to the State Governments, we find substantially the same state of things. The terms of the offices are very short, and the incumbents are re-eligible. The number of aspirants *always* in the field will necessarily be in proportion to the shortness of the terms of office; because the chances of success will occur more frequently. When an aspirant fails to obtain a nomination at one convention, he has only to wait a short time for another; and this keeps him always hopeful and always on hand. For this reason, the genuine demagogue is always in favor of short terms.

The legitimate effect of short terms is to swell the number of unscrupulous aspirants, and to increase the number of delinquencies in office. When an aspirant succeeds in obtaining office, he finds that it has cost him one of his two years' salary to reach the position ; and he is, therefore, powerfully tempted to steal to make up his losses. True, the power of impeachment hangs over him ; but he knows that this power is rarely if ever enforced, because his term is likely to expire before the charges could be investigated, if made ; and that the people, if aware of his delinquency, will comfort themselves with the reflection that his term will soon be out, and they will replace him by a more honest man. But the new incumbent comes into office under the same circumstances, and liable to the same temptations. Even when the officer is honest,.he is often, if not generally, rendered weak and vaccillating. If called upon to execute the law upon influential men, or upon any considerable number of voters, he finds himself placed in this perplexing predicament. If he does his duty, he is almost certain to offend a sufficient number of his own party to defeat his renomination. When his name comes before the convention, every other aspirant will be opposed to him, because they will not wish, if nominated, to have their names associated with his. " He is a good fellow," they will say, " and has strictly done his duty ; but he is unfortunate, and cannot be elected. It is useless to nominate him. It would defeat the whole ticket." The result is, that the honest officer fails because he did his duty. Time and oft experience have shown this to be true. The poor officer finds himself placed between two fires. If he does his duty, he is beaten ; and if he does it not, it is still the same. He therefore hesitates, temporizes, and makes efforts to compromise, until he finally renders the law itself ridiculous, and destroys, in the minds of the people, all due respect for it. We have seen the effect of these causes upon the action of the national and State executives, and upon the officers of both governments, except the judges of the Federal courts.*

---

* By the second section of the second article of the Constitution, the President is made commander-in-chief of the militia of the several States when called into the actual service of the United States ; but by a provision of the eighth section of the first article, the power to appoint the officers is reserved to the States respectively.

The idea of giving the chief command to the President, and at the same time leaving it in the power of the States to appoint the officers he is required to command, would seem incompatible with due subordination and efficiency. We now see the effects of this State power of appointment in the fact that so many mere politicians are

The influence of party spirit is potently felt in all the ramifications of society, and has most materially affected the administration of justice in our country. Very few men of wealth or of popularity have been convicted of murder, or other serious offence, in the United States. Hamilton, a wealthy man, was convicted and executed some years ago in Kentucky, for the murder of Dr. Sanderson, another wealthy man; and Dr. Webster, a man of literary reputation, suffered in Massachusetts for the murder of Dr. Parkman, who was a wealthy and prominent man. But the instances have been few; and none, so far as known, where the murdered victim was an obscure individual, without friends or influence. · Of politicians, no instances of conviction are remembered. Partisan influence is powerful; and of bank and other corporation delinquents, there is not one in a hundred ever punished. Escape is almost, if not entirely, universal.

The effect of the short terms of office, and of the re-eligibility of incumbents, is plainly seen in the general licentiousness of the press. All parties, cliques, and prominent aspirants for important positions, have their organs, which are under their control, and but reflect the party bitterness and personal feelings of those who dictate the contents and tone of their editorials. These causes have led to a vast increase in the number of newspapers; but in proportion as the number increases, their character depreciates.

§ 15. *An elective judiciary.*

The last conservative element in the State Governments has been destroyed by making the judiciary elective. Since this has been done, candidates for seats upon the bench are nomi-

---

appointed to the most important military positions. This was to have been expected. The Governors in whom the power of appointment is vested, hold their offices but for short terms, are eligible for other terms, and of course find it hard to rise above their party friendships and political associations. They will not easily forget the services of those politicians to whose efforts they owe their own positions, and upon whose assistance they rely for further promotion or continuance in office.

But the deplorable result is, that the army must bleed, and the country suffer, for the want of military capacity in these officers. The field of battle is no place for mere political combinations. Nothing but genuine merit can bear the test of that stern and rigid trial.

nated by political conventions; and without such nomination, no candidate could succeed, though he possessed the character and qualifications of Chief Justice Marshall.

The evils of such a theory are not well understood by the great mass of voters, and cannot be stated but in part here. The essence, however, of all the objections against it, consists in taking judicial questions from the proper forum, and, in *practical* effect, submitting them to the discussion of a crowd. The evils of the theory have not yet fully appeared; but in the progress of time, they will swell to gigantic proportions.

The first result will be to place political demagogues upon the bench; men who, during the canvass, will freely intimate to certain influential parties their opinions upon certain exciting and important judicial questions, in reference to which there exists a great diversity of interests in the community. And when the candidate becomes the judge, he is still eligible for re-election, always an aspirant upon the bench, and always electioneering. A case comes up before him, where the law is clearly one way, and the opinions and interests of the masses the other way. How is he to decide? and how will a demagogue decide? If he decides against public opinion, he loses his seat. The question is one in which he is directly and personally concerned; and he is practically made a judge in his own case, because the practical result, *to him*, is the same. In sustaining public opinion, for the time he sustains his own immediate interests; but by the time the next election comes around, public opinion has changed, and he must change with it.

The theory of an elective judiciary is studiously designed to subject judges to the greatest temptations, and their strict integrity to the severest trials, without any practical or efficient check; for when a man without integrity has public opinion to sustain him, he feels pretty safe. The evils of the theory would be manifest to all the world, if the true state of facts could always be known. Suppose, for example, a candidate for a seat upon the bench should pledge himself, *in advance*, to decide certain judicial questions in a certain way; and suppose, after election, a case involving the principle should come before him, and the lawyer upon the opposite side should propose to discuss the question. The judge, if candid, should say: " Mr. ——, I cannot hear argument upon this question, because it would be idle to do so. I have pledged myself, in advance, to my constituents, to decide this question against you, and I must keep my pledge to them, though it may be true that you are in the right, and could plainly make it appear. But as the matter *now* stands, this Court does not, in fact, decide cases itself, but simply records the judgments of public opinion for the time being. I am sorry for you and your client; but I love myself better than I love the law of this case, and I could not have been elected unless I had made the pledge I did; and I was bound to be elected. That was the great end for which I struggled." *

---

* The history of England shows conclusively that the administration of justice never can be pure until the judges are made independent. So long as the judges of the English Judiciary were removable by the crown, they were its slaves, with a few noble exceptions. During the reign of Henry VIII., Cromwell "asked of the judges whether, if Parliament should condemn a man to die for treason without hearing him, the attainder could not be disputed? They answered that it was a dangerous question, and that Parliament should rather set an example to inferior courts by proceeding according to justice. But being pressed to reply by the king's express commandment, they said that an attainder in Parliament, whether the party had been heard or not in his defence, could never be reversed in a court of law." It is remarkable that Cromwell was himself the first victim.—(Hallam's Con. His., 28, 29.)

As to the judges under Elizabeth, Mr. Hallam says :

"I have found it impossible not to anticipate, in more places than one, some of those glaring transgressions of natural as well as positive law, that rendered our courts of justice in cases of treason little better than the caverns of murderers. Whoever was arraigned at their bar was almost certain to meet a virulent prosecution, a judge hardly distinguishable from the prosecutor except by his ermine, and a passive, pusillanimous jury."—(Con. His., 138.)

Under James I. the judges were no better. "The courts of justice, it is hardly necessary to say, did not consist of men conscientiously impartial between the king and the subject ; some corrupt with hope of promotion, many more fearful of removal, or awe-struck by the frowns of power."—(Id., 184.) In the case of Peacham, "the king directed Bacon previously to confer with the judges of the King's Bench, one by one, in order to secure their determination for the crown." The prisoner was convicted, but died in prison.—(Id., 198.)

In some few instances, constituting mere *exceptions* to the general conduct of the judges, they manifested a noble spirit.

"They unanimously declared, when Charles I. expressed a desire that Felton, the assassin of the Duke of Buckingham, might be put to the rack in order to make him discover his accomplices, that the law of England did not allow the use of torture."—(Id., 243.)

In the case of Hampden, there were two of the twelve judges who manifested a most intrepid spirit, namely : Hutton and Croke. Of the latter, Mr. Hallam says :

"Croke, whose conduct on the bench in other political questions was not without blemish, had resolved to give judgment for the king, but was withheld by his wife,

But even when the judge is immovable, and above the influence of personal considerations, and always ready and willing to lose his seat rather than stultify himself, he is placed in a very delicate and painful position, when his motives are open to plausible and continued suspicion and reproach. The public newspaper press is generally edited by men who have a little legal learning, (a dangerous thing when just enough to mislead,) and will discuss, in their columns, the decisions of the courts, and condemn or approve, as the supposed opinion of their readers, or their own inaccurate judgments may dictate. Every extraneous and outside influence is brought to bear upon the Court. And not only so, but the judge must necessarily employ much of his time in making political combinations, or he must fail to receive a renomination by the convention of the party to which he himself belongs. Unless he do so, his opponent, not being on the bench, and against whose judicial opinions nothing can be said, because of them nothing is publicly known, (though known to the influential few,) will have greatly the advantage over him in the convention. All his opponent has to do to defeat him, under such circumstances, is to spend about six months' time in bringing out, in different counties, his own particular friends, as aspirants to seats in the convention.

The theory of an elective judiciary not only ultimately, as a general rule, excludes the best men from the bench, and puts political demagogues in their places, but its tendency is to degrade the bar itself. Although district courts are but subordinate tribunals, the judges of these courts have it in their power to favor or oppress particular attorneys to a great extent. When an attorney becomes unpopular with the court, he loses his practice, because parties litigant will not employ him at the

who implored him not to sacrifice his conscience for fear of any danger or prejudice to his family, being content to suffer any misery with him, rather than to be an occasion for him to violate his integrity."—(Id., 251, note.)

This noble woman, greater than her husband, should be had "in eternal remembrance."

As to the judges during the reign of Charles II., "Never were our tribunals so disgraced by the brutal manners and iniquitous partiality of the bench as in the latter years of this reign."—(Id., 471.)

The independence of the judges was secured by the Act of Settlement. Since then "no judge can be dismissed from office, except in consequence of a conviction for some offence, or the address of both houses of Parliament, which is tantamount to an Act of the Legislature."—(Id., 597.)

5

risk, real or imaginary, of losing their cases. This state of things has a strong influence upon many members of the profession; and hence they become obsequious flatterers and supporters of unworthy aspirants. For example, two men are aspirants or candidates for the bench. A is a man above the influence of prejudice or revenge; but B is a man who never forgets or forgives an opponent. The members of the bar have to choose between them. The vote is likely to be a close one. Each member of the bar puts this dilemma to himself: "If I vote against A, and he should be elected, I can lose nothing; but if I oppose B, and he should be elected, he will never forgive the act, though he may never allude to it." Such considerations will have their influence with many lawyers.

It may, with truth, be said, that the members of the bar are almost, if not quite, universally opposed to an elective judiciary. The writer has never met a lawyer of respectable attainments that did not decidedly condemn the elective theory; nor has he met anywhere with many intelligent men of any class or profession, that did not agree with the bar in this view. The opinion of the bar, upon a question of this character, is justly entitled to great weight. If the members of the profession do not understand the science of government, they understand nothing. As a class, they have every reason for sustaining a just, speedy, and economical administration of justice. Errors, delays, and extravagant costs, keep parties out of court, and are clearly an injury to the profession. The members of the bar have, therefore, every professional, honorable, and just motive to sustain *only* the best mode of choosing judges. The higher and purer the administration of justice, the more honorable and profitable to the noble profession to which they belong.

The most intelligent and conservative men in the nation have always known that our theory was but an *experiment*. They have, therefore, watched its progress with deep concern; and, most unhappily, they have had no cause to put aside their doubts and fears. The theory has not grown more conservative, (as it should have done,) in proportion as our population increased and our territory extended; but has rapidly and continually grown more and more radical. It seems, in its very nature, to be especially adapted to create and foster *mere politicians*, while it is death to true statesmen, who, as a general rule, are left in private life. And these increasing evils seem to admit of no remedy. The people themselves are so hampered and carried away by party spirit, that appeals to them are very rarely successful. True, they occasionally, at long intervals, arouse themselves, and, in their short-lived wrath, hurl the mere politicians from power; but these spasmodic efforts readily exhaust themselves, the waves of public indignation quickly subside, and things soon resume their accustomed state. It is like casting a stone into a stream, which act occasions a temporary bubble, and then the current flows on again as ever.*

And this state of things is not so much the fault of the people, as of the theory itself. Men will differ in their views of political questions, and must, of necessity, divide themselves into political parties; and when once so divided, regard to principle and consistency will force even the unaspiring masses to vote for persons representing their own views. Hence they are obliged, by stress of circumstances, to resort to party machinery; and when they do this, they are compelled, in due time, to be controlled by demagogues. "Eternal vigilance," said Mr. Jefferson, "is the price of liberty;" but this "eternal vigilance" in attending, *so often*, both *primary* and *final* elections, is a costly effort to the toiling millions; and though "*eternal*," it is not, in itself, competent to detect the secret springs by which conventions are practically moved.

---

* Perhaps no instance in our history more forcibly shows the overpowering influence which even public prejudice will have over political men under our theory, than the melancholy case of Alexander Hamilton. Col. Benton justly says: "Hard was the fate of Hamilton." It was hard, indeed; not so much for the fact that he fell in the prime of life, but that he died in consequence of deliberately committing an act which his conscience and judgment condemned; and this under the specious pretence of expediency. He was utterly opposed to duelling, and yet he fought. In his own words, his reasons were these:

"The ability to be in future useful, whether in resisting mischief or effecting good, in those crises of our public affairs which seem likely to happen, would probably be inseparable from a conformity with prejudice in this particular."

It is a great misfortune that a great man, in an enlightened age, should reason in this way. That evil should be done that good may come of it, is a short-sighted view of principle, as well as of consequences. We can well understand how an individual who regards the practice of duelling as correct in itself, can be engaged in a duel. He acts consistently; but for a man deliberately to do wrong, simply to satisfy others, shows great weakness. Is a community which requires a man to violate his conscientious principles worthy to be served by a just man? A great and good man should be content when he is in the right, whether others think so or not; and no man should or can be happy, when he violates his own conscience.

CHAPTER III.

THE ULTIMATE REMEDY.

§ 1. *The ultimate remedy stated.*

A WRITER who objects to things as they are, should suggest a remedy for the alleged evils to which his objections refer. To simply complain, without being able to point out any remedy, is to gratify a mere fault-finding disposition; and this is doing an idle, if not a vicious thing. The writer will endeavor to comply with the reasonable duty incumbent upon those who make objections.

In assigning the alleged defects of our governmental theory, as the fundamental causes of the present crisis in the affairs of the Nation, the proposed ultimate and permanent remedy has been already incidentally suggested. This remedy consists in removing the causes themselves; and to do this, the theory of the Government must be thoroughly and radically amended. Partial and temporary remedies are deceptive. They may give relief for a time, only to be followed by evils more distressing than ever. We must go back and begin at the beginning, and profit by our later and more dearly-bought experience. It is a rule of logic, that errors should be corrected in the places where they occur. With a fresh, ample, and fertile territory, and, comparatively, a sparse population, and, consequently, a people generally free from want, and, for that reason, virtuous and independent, our theory succeeded very well at the beginning. But as, in the national progress of things, our circumstances approached the condition of the populations of the Old World, the practical defects of our theory became more and more apparent.*

---

* Malthus assumes these positions as true:

" The increase of population is necessarily limited by the means of subsistence.

" Population invariably increases when the means of subsistence increases, unless prevented by powerful and obvious checks.

" These checks, and the checks which keep the population down to the level of the means of subsistence, are moral restraint, vice, and misery.

" Corn countries are more populous than pasture countries, and rice countries more populous than corn countries."—(Malthus *on Population*, vol. i., 532-4.)

The theory should be amended in these three general respects:

1. It should be made more simple.

There is no governmental theory in the world so complex as our own. This is agreed to by all our jurists and statesmen. All *avoidable* complexity should be excluded from the theory. It should be made as simple as the great and various purposes of government will allow. Government, at best, is a vast and complex machine ; but like the machinery of a great steamship, though complex, it should be harmonious in its operations.

2. It should be made more conservative.

The acute and profound Mons. De Tocqueville, in his able work upon America, very justly says :

" In conformity with this principle, America is, at the present day, the country in the world where laws last the shortest time."—(p. 278.)

Few countries have suffered so much from hasty, changeable, and excessive legislation as our own. We have not, in our rushing mad pursuit of objects before us, stopped to secure the steps already taken. Majorities alternate in our country as elsewhere ; and in our theory there are no efficient checks upon the interests and passions of mere majorities, for the time being. The same elegant writer remarks upon this unchecked power of present majorities, as follows :

" The majority, therefore, in that country exercise a prodigious actual authority, and a moral influence scarcely less preponderant ; no obstacles exist which can impede, or so much as retard its progress, or which can induce it to heed the complaints of those whom it crushes upon its path. This state of things is fatal in itself and dangerous for the future."—(p. 277.)

3. It should be made stronger.

The Federal Government is too weak, and there are too many restrictions upon its powers, in view of the extent of our country, its varied productions, antagonistic interests, and differ-ent domestic institutions. There is no government less worthy of the respect of mankind, and of the obedience of those whom it mocks with a farcical rule and protection, than that which is impotent to accomplish the very ends for which government is alone instituted. A strong government may oppress its people ;

but it, at least, gives them protection as against foreign enemies, and as against each other.

"The circumstances," says Hamilton, "that endanger the safety of nations are infinite; and for this reason, no constitutional shackles can wisely be imposed on the power to which the care of it is committed. This power ought to be coextensive with all the possible combinations of such circumstances; and ought to be under the direction of the councils which are appointed to preside over the common defence."

This was said in reference to the power "to raise armies; to build and equip fleets; to prescribe rules for the government of both; to direct their operations; to provide for their support." In reference to the extent of our territory, he said:

"This, at all events, must be evident, that the very difficulty itself, drawn from the extent of the country, is the strongest argument in favor of an energetic government; for any other can certainly never preserve the union of so large an empire."—(*Federalist*, No 23.)

It is very true that these observations of Hamilton were made in answer to the objection, that too much power had been conferred upon the Federal Government by the Constitution. But when it is remembered that he was decidedly in favor of a much stronger form of government, his remarks may justly be taken in a more general sense. The heading of the number from which these extracts are taken, is in these words: "The necessity of a government, at least equally energetic with the one proposed."

The great end to be accomplished, is to combine strength in the Government with security and liberty in the governed, so far as this can be done. To accomplish this end, restrictions upon the powers of government are not *generally* so safe, and at the same time efficient, as their proper *distribution* among different departments, which act as checks upon each other. "I repeat here," says the same great statesman, "what I have observed in substance in another place, that all observations, founded upon the danger of usurpation, ought to be referred to the composition and structure of the government, not to the nature and extent of its powers."—(*Federalist*, No. 31.)

§ 2. *There should be no State sovereignty.*

The States should be strictly subordinate corporations, and only permitted to exercise such powers as may be allowed by Congress. In other words, they should possess no sovereignty, in fact or in theory, and should bear to the Government substantially the same relation that Territorial governments now bear to that of the Union. The acts of their legislatures should be only *prima facie* valid, and be subject to the negative of Congress. The Governor of each State should be appointed by the President, by and with the advice and consent of the Senate, and should hold his office at the pleasure of the President. He should have a qualified negative upon the bills of the State Legislature, which should be composed of a Senate and House of Representatives. Members of the State Senate should be elected by the people of their respective senatorial districts, and should hold their positions for life, subject to the right of expulsion by their own body ; and members of the House of Representatives should be elected by the people of their respective counties, and for a term of four years. The appointment of all subordinate executive and ministerial State officers should be vested in the Governor, except those of municipalities.

Such an amendment would relieve our theory of that political monster—a divided sovereignty. Every citizen would then *plainly* know the government to which his allegiance was rightfully due. He would not then be placed in the painful and illogical predicament, of having to love and serve two different supremes, of contrary wills. He could not then, as now, by the same act, commit two different offences ; and thus be subjected to double punishment. It would then be out of the power of fathers to teach their sons, and of politicians to persuade the people, that their superior allegiance was due to the State. Rebellion would then be *plain, unmistakable* rebellion ; and not, as now, a forcible attempt upon plausible grounds, to sustain alleged Constitutional rights. The theory of our Government would then be simple. It would be harmonious in theory and practice.

The vast amount of time heretofore consumed, in all the Courts and Legislative Assemblies, State and National, and by our law writers, politicians, and statesmen, in discussing the multiplied and perplexing questions, continually arising, regarding the respective constitutional powers of the Federal and State Governments, would then be saved. Any one who will examine the subject, will see the amount of labor, time, and intellect heretofore consumed in these discussions. Should the present theory continue half a century longer, it is difficult to conceive how Congress and the Federal Courts could possibly despatch the business before them. This evil has become one of great magnitude.

This illogical attempt to divide sovereignty, has mainly given rise to the bitter and intemperate discussions in Congress, so injurious to our feelings as a people, and to our honor at home and abroad. It has also led to the most deplorable results among the people themselves. Their bitterness is but the reflection of that engendered in Congress and in the State Legislatures. Grievances, real or imaginary, will arise from time to time, under the best, and the best administered government in the world. Even measures substantially just under the circumstances, will bear harder upon one class, or upon one section, than upon another. These partial evils cannot be avoided by human wisdom.

This being true, the misfortune of our theory is, that these evils can generally be plausibly imputed to violations of the Constitution—to encroachments upon State rights—to an invasion of State sovereignty. And when a citizen is once convinced that the Constitutional rights of *his* State have been invaded, he feels indignant; and when satisfied that this invasion has been deliberate, and continued for any considerable period of time, and that it will, in all probability, become permanent, all his energies and resentments are aroused, his soul is stirred within him, and his hatred of his supposed oppressor becomes, in time, so intense, that he is ready to die a martyr to that which he believes to be *the* right.

These temptations to forcible resistance, under the name of defending the Constitution, should be removed. We should have a governmental theory, simple and clear enough in its main features—those that are fundamental—so that the good sense of every man can understand, at least, what officers he is bound to obey. We should not be left in doubt as to our rightful master. We are ready to give due obedience. It is both our interest and our duty. Our judgments and our hearts tell us so. We are willing and anxious to be governed; because we regard legitimate government, not as a curse, but as a blessing. But give us only one master. We cannot have and serve *two*.

§ 3. *The Executive Power.*

The Executive power of the Nation should be vested in a President, who should be a native citizen of the United States, and be elected by a direct vote of the people. He should hold his office for a term of twenty years, be ineligible for a second term, incapable of holding any other office, and subject to removal by impeachment. All officers appointed by him, except judicial, should hold their offices during his pleasure. He should have, besides, the right to demand the written opinions of all heads of departments, a Cabinet to consist of the Secretaries of State, of the Treasury, and of War, and the Attorney-general, who should be entitled to seats in the House of Representatives, but without the right to vote. In addition to the other powers conferred upon him by the present Constitution, and those mentioned above, he should have the power to declare martial law, and to suspend the privilege of the writ of *habeas corpus*, for a limited period, during the recess of Congress.

It may be objected, and with much reason, that an elective Executive can never entirely escape from the influence of those aspirants for office under him, to whose efforts he is mainly indebted for his own elevation to power; and that an hereditary Executive is the only one that can avoid the influence of party spirit, as he comes into office without pledges or obligations, either expressed or implied. It may also be said, that an elective theory is more apt to give rise to frequent civil wars.

It must be conceded that both theories are liable to *some* objections. The theory of an hereditary Executive is certain to place in power a greater number of incompetent and unworthy persons. The history of France, England, and other monarchies will show, that the hereditary theory does not lessen the dangers of civil war. Frequent and bloody civil wars have occurred in struggles for the succession. Questions of legitimacy often arise, exceedingly difficult to determine. Governments have been perplexed, and nations wasted, because it could not be certainly known, whether a particular marriage was legal or otherwise. If legal, one claimant would be the rightful heir to the crown ; if illegal, then the other. These discussions are often of a very painful and indelicate character ; and every correct theory of government should give no cause for them.

Besides, the danger of civil war, under the theory of an elective Executive, arises mainly from the fact, that the incumbent is eligible for another term. He being a candidate for another term, and being in possession of the office, and in command of the army and navy, and these being large in proportion to the entire population, and the race being sufficiently close to give rise to plausible doubt as to which competitor is really entitled to the office, it is easy, in such cases, to make charges of fraud in the election ; and, as fraud vitiates every thing, a plausible case may be made out by the incumbent, who will not hesitate to use his power over the army and navy, and over his party friends, to retain power. But when the incumbent is plainly limited to a single term, this danger cannot arise from any defect in the theory. It would be a case of *plain usurpation*.

A very grave and serious objection to the theory of an hereditary Executive is, that the people are often made to bleed and suffer, simply to gratify the pride and personal resentment of the monarch. The pages of history are full of such instances. Royal families necessarily connect themselves with those of other countries by marriage, and thus form family alliances, often very detrimental to their own governments.

It will be obvious, upon reflection, that the long term of the Presidential office, will avoid most of the evils of the present theory. It must be conceded, that candidates for that office would most likely be nominated by conventions, as heretofore ; but the futility of requiring aspirants to commit themselves *so long* in advance, to any particular line of policy, must be apparent. The long term would more likely lead to the selection of better men. The new President, when once in power, is placed in an independent position, has no hopes of future promotion himself, and no plausible excuse for sweeping removals, for mere political reasons. The long term before him will allow him to wait for vacancies occasioned by deaths, resignations, and removals for cause. The operation of the executive power would be steady, energetic, and consistent. The President would have time to deliberately adopt and successfully carry out his measures. The power of impeachment would not only be the more promptly enforced, but the fear of forfeiting his long term of office, would deter even an incumbent of doubtful integrity from any gross violation of duty. The theory of long terms of office has these very decisive advantages : 1. It gives the incumbent ample time to make himself thoroughly acquainted with the duties of his position ; 2. It removes the temptation to delinquency ; 3. It is a powerful check upon it.

A President placed in that secure position would have nothing to fear while he did right. He would have ample time and opportunity to make himself a true statesman, and every motive to lay a solid foundation for deserved and enduring fame, in a vigorous, honest, and. wise administration. The mere passions and excitements of the hour would not often influence his action. Placed above party trammels, and beyond the reach of party and sectional prejudice, his administration would not only be good in itself, but it would command the confidence and respect of the people, from the absence of all motive to do wrong. Under the practical operation of such a theory, we should have every reason to expect a long succession of illustrious men in the highest office in the world.

It is a matter of great practical importance, that the ordinary advisory body of the Executive should not be too large ; because it is not safe to intrust the keeping of Cabinet secrets to many persons ; and it is not convenient to assemble and consult so many as often as may be required. Even large advisory bodies move slowly. It is also of great practical importance that members of the Cabinet should be allowed seats in the House of Representatives, so that the President may propose his measures through them, and sustain those measures by argument and explanation. In legislating for a great nation, time is very important, and moments become valuable. Every facility, therefore, for expediting business, and for the conviction and prevention of errors in legislation, should be adopted. The members of the Cabinet, being familiar with the views of the President, could at once, in many cases, afford that information, which it now requires resolution of inquiry to obtain. So, the members of the Cabinet, being also acquainted with the *practical* operation of the laws, the business of the principal departments, and the existing state of legislation, would be more competent to draw up bills for many purposes, than the regular members themselves. Many of the perplexing errors now found in Acts of Congress would be thus avoided. There is nothing more difficult than to frame a bill upon a complex subject, and yet have the bill full, clear, concise, and consistent.

In a country so extensive and diversified as ours, it is important to the national safety, and the best ultimate humanity, that the President should have the power to declare martial law, and to suspend the privilege of the writ of habeas corpus, in cases of invasion, insurrection, rebelli&n, and for a limited time, during the recess of Congress. The late distressing events in our country, have shown the wisdom and necessity of such a provision. There is no means more efficient, and at the same time more humane in suppressing insurrection or rebellion, than the power of promptly arresting and imprisoning suspected individuals. It *separates* the leaders to whom the secrets of the plot are alone confided, confuses their plans of operation, dispirits their adherents, and often prevents the dire necessity of shedding blood. In the midst of military operations, there is no time to issue writs of habeas corpus, and calmly investigate the alleged causes of imprisonment. No doubt mistakes and abuses must and will occur, and innocent persons suffer *for a time*. But when the peace and safety of the government are at stake, individuals had better suffer *temporary* wrong, in *some* cases, than that a greater evil should befal an entire community. The maxim of the law, that it is better that ninety-nine guilty should escape, than that one innocent person should suffer, is often carried too far, and is not applicable to the extreme case where the nation is in peril.

It is very true that the English people are so jealous of their personal liberty, that the power to suspend the privilege of the writ of habeas corpus is *alone* reserved to Parliament. (1 Black. Com. 136.) But the reasons for this restriction upon the powers of the crown would not exist with us. The king holds his crown for life, with succession to *his* heirs, and is not criminally responsible for *any act whatever*. The English Constitution leaves him without sufficient checks, and with many inducements to increase his powers. In the hands of the crown, the power of suspension would be highly dangerous. But the President would hold his office for a single term, without succession, and subject to impeachment. He would, therefore, have no motive for the wilful abuse of the power, and the danger of impeachment would operate as a powerful check upon him.

There can be no doubt that, under the existing Constitution, the power of suspension is alone vested in Congress. This is conclusively shown by Chief Justice Taney, in his opinion delivered in the late case of ex parte John Merryman. *As a judge*, the Chief Justice could only declare the law as *it is;* not as, in *his* opinion, *it should be.* But the necessity for the existence of this power in the President, during the recess of Congress, has led to violations of the present Constitution by some of our military officers, whose acts have been overlooked upon the ground of necessity. But the plea of necessity is a dangerous precedent to indulge under a government of *limited* powers.

It may be said by some, that it would be better for the President to hold his office during good behavior, rather than for the long and fixed term of twenty years. But this is objectionable, because it makes the periods of election irregular. The people should always know with certainty, and long in advance, when they are to exercise the privilege of electing their President. They would thus have ample time for discussion and reflection. Besides, it would become necessary that the vacancy should be filled temporarily, until the result of the election could be known ; and this would increase the interruptions in the administration of this department, and render its policy more fluctuating and unsteady.

The Vice-President should possess the same qualifications, and be elected at the same time, and for the same term, as the President. The Vice-President should possess the powers conferred upon the office by the present Constitution. Provisions for filling vacancies in the office of President and Vice-President should be the same as at present.

§ 4. *The Legislative Power.*

The Legislative power should be vested in a Congress, to consist of a Senate and House of Representatives. Members of the Senate should be chosen in the mode now adopted, but should retain their seats for life, subject to expulsion by their own body, and should be incapable of holding any other position. Members of the House should be elected by the people of their respective districts for the term of four years. The Senate and House should possess the same *relative* powers as at present.

A Senate thus composed would be the most dignified, illustrious, and justly conservative body in the world. The members would have ample time and opportunity, and every inducement, to make of themselves true statesmen. Their attention would not be occupied with conflicts between duty and ambition. They would have but ONE thing to do, and would be beyond the reach of passion, prejudice, or personal interest. Their fame could only be based upon real merit. No political combinations could add any thing to their reputations. To be a life-long and distinguished member of such a body would be ample to gratify reasonable ambition.

Such a body would be superior to the English House of Lords, in several material respects: 1. The House of Lords represents only certain classes of the conservative element of the nation, while the Senate would represent all. 2. The House of Lords, as a body, would be inferior in capacity, owing to the elements of which it is composed. The hereditary peers are not generally distinguished for ability. The same is true of the Bishops, whose profession does not make them practical statesmen.

The provision that renders Senators incapable of all further promotion, is a very important one, and would not only exclude all topics of personal dispute, but would give the action of such a venerable body the most deserved weight with the people. There being no motive of interest or feeling to sway the judgment of Senators, (a majority of whom would, at all times, possess ample character, experience, and capacity,) there could, in most cases, be no plausible ground for objection to their action. Every man in the nation would have just reason to repose confidence in such a body of statesmen. The time of that body would not be consumed, as now, in discussing the political pretensions and antecedents of aspiring Senators for the Presidency, and often in fierce personal quarrels. The cause being removed, the melancholy effect would cease.*

The members of the House of Representatives would be fresh from the people, and would, therefore, represent the progressive

* The history of the proceedings of the Senate will show a number of cases where Senators were evidently influenced, to a great extent, by personal ambition. Perhaps the most noted case was the rejection of Mr. Van Buren as minister to England. Col. Benton, in his Thirty Years' View, gives the secret history of that rejection ; according to which account the leading motive of those who voted against the nomination was the desire to kill off a competitor for the Presidency, who was in the way of Messrs. Clay, Calhoun, and Webster. "Rejection of the nomination was not enough—a killing off in the public mind was intended ; and therefore the unusual process of the elaborate preparation and the intended publication of the speeches." All the speakers abjured all sinister motives. "The acccomplished Forsyth complimented, in a way to be perfectly understood, this excess of patriotism, which could voluntarily inflict so much self-distress for the sake of the public good ; and I, most unwittingly, brought the misery of one of the gentlemen to a sudden and ridiculous conclusion by a chance remark. It was Mr. Gabriel Moore, of Alabama, who sat near me, and to whom I said, when the vote was declared : 'You have broken a minister, and elected a Vice-President.' He asked me how ; and I told him the people would see nothing in it but a combination of rivals against a competitor, and would pull them all down and set him up. 'Good God !' said he, 'why didn't you tell me that before I voted, and I would have voted the other way.'" In Mr. Moore's speech, only delivered a few moments before this, is to be found this passage : "Sir, it is proper that I should declare that the evidence adduced against the character and conduct of the late Secretary of State, and the sources from which this evidence emanates, have made an impression on my mind that will require of me, in the conscientious though painful discharge of my duty, to record my vote against his nomination.' I heard Mr. Calhoun say to one of his doubting friends, 'It will kill him, sir—kill him dead. He will never kick, sir—never kick !' and the alacrity with which he gave the casting votes, on the two occasions, both vital, on which they were put into his hands, attested the sincerity of his belief, and his readiness for the work." A tie vote was purposely produced twice, by the surplus votes against the nomination going out, and Mr. Calhoun, then being Vice-President, was thus compelled to give the casting vote and show his position. In reference to this case, Col. Benton also says :

"The famous Madame Roland, when mounting the scaffold, apostrophized the mock statue upon it with this exclamation : 'Oh Liberty ! how many crimes are committed in thy name !' After what I have seen during my thirty years of inside and outside views in the Congress of the United States, I feel qualified to paraphrase the apostrophe, and exclaim : 'Oh Politics ! how much bamboozling is practised in thy game ! '"—(Thirty Years' View, vol. i., 214.)

But whether we give full credence to the history of this transaction or not, as given by Col. Benton, Senators (especially all those known or supposed to have aspirations for further promotion) are placed in a very delicate and embarrassing position. In cases like the one mentioned, there may be ample reason for rejecting the nomination ; and yet Senators would be deterred from so voting, because it would subject their motives to plausible imputation, and in the end promote the political rise of the unworthy nominee.

element of the nation. The term of four years would seem
preferable to that of two, as it would give members a reasonable
time to make themselves fully acquainted with the rules of the
House, and the exising state of legislation. The present term
of two years is too short, considering the extent of our country
and the complex character of its diversified interests. A member
can now scarcely prepare himself so as properly to *introduce*
his measures before his time is out.*

A body constituted as the House of Representatives, is indispensably necessary to arouse the attention and quicken the
action of the conservative branch. There is great practical danger
that, without this fresh, young, and vigorous body, the
Senate would become too conservative. But as the Senate
would have every motive to do right, and none to do wrong,
the persistent assertion of true principles and the advocacy of
correct measures on the part of the House, could not fail, in
due time, to secure the consent of the Senate. The correctness
of this opinion is proven by the history of English legislation,
where the House of Lords, from the nature of its structure and
composition, is more apt to be swayed by the interests and
habits of particular classes than would be the Senate ; and for
that reason, offers a greater obstacle to the passage of just and
liberal measures. It required some forty years' hard exertion
of Earl Grey and Major Cartwright to carry British Parliamentary reform, and long-continued exertions to carry Catholic
emancipation, corn-law repeal, abolition of the slave-trade, and
other great measures. But the Senate, from its composition,
would be much more susceptible to the appeals of reason and
justice.

§ 5. *The Judiciary.*

The judges of all the more important courts of record should
be appointed by the President, by and with the advice and consent of the Senate ; and the judges of the courts of inferior im-

* " Short service and not popular election, is the evil of the House of Representatives ; and this becomes more apparent by contrast—contrast between the North and
the South—the caucus, or rotatory system, not prevailing in the South, and useful
members being usually continued from that quarter as long as useful ; and thus, with
fewer members, usually showing a greater number of men who have attained a distinction."—(Thirty Years' View, vol. i., 207.)

portance by the Governors of the States, by and with the advice and consent of the State Senates. Both classes of judges should hold their offices during good behavior, and be subject to removal from office by impeachment. The judges of the Supreme Court of the United States should be incapable of holding any other position. A seat upon the bench of that Court should be held sufficient to satisfy human ambition.

A Supreme Court, thus constituted, would be superior to the Court of King's Bench in England. Though the judges there have now fixed salaries, and are not removable at the pleasure of the crown as formerly, they are subject to removal simply upon the address of both Houses of Parliament, and are under the influence of the hope of future promotion. In reference to the English judges, Mr. Hallam remarks:

"It is always to be kept in mind that they are still accessible to the hope of further promotion, to the zeal of political attachment, to the flattery of princes and ministers; that the bias of their prejudices, as elderly and peaceable men, will, in a plurality of cases, be on the side of power; that they have very frequently been trained, as advocates, to vindicate every proceeding of the crown; from all which we should look on them with some little vigilance, and not come hastily to the conclusion that, because their commissions cannot be vacated by the crown's authority, they are wholly out of the reach of its influence."—(Con. His., 597.)

§ 6. *Salaries.*

The President, the heads of the Executive departments, judges of the Courts, and members of Congress, should receive fixed salaries, which should not be increased or diminished during the term for which they were appointed. As to the salaries of the President, heads of departments, and judges of the Courts, the Constitution itself should provide that they should be paid out of the first moneys in the Treasury, without the necessity of any appropriation by Congress for that purpose.

This provision is important to render the Executive and Judicial departments independent of a factious House of Representatives; as in this House all revenue and appropriation bills would originate, a factious majority of its members, driven by party exasperation, might withhold the appropriations for the other departments. It is well to remove this temptation from the House. One department should not have the power over the means of living of the principal officers of the other two. The very object of a Constitutional theory is to distribute the powers of Government among independent departments. Therefore, to make one department dependent upon another is to defeat the very purpose of a free Constitution.

§ 7. *Slavery.*

This vexed question has been so much discussed, and often in a spirit so bitter, and so intense a feeling now exists in reference to it, that but a single remark seems proper under this head. Whatever settlement of the question should be finally adopted, should be plainly stated in the Constitution ; and when thus stated, both sections of the Union might rely, with entire confidence, that the guarantees of the Constitution would be faithfully preserved, by a Government constituted as the one proposed.

§ 8. *Conclusion.*

The causes which are alleged to have produced the present crisis, and the proposed ultimate remedy, have now been stated. Though the question of slavery has often been placed in the foreground, it is but a secondary, and not a fundamental cause. Had that question constituted the fundamental difficulty, more earnest efforts would have been made to settle it. But the best minds in the nation have lost faith in the practical efficiency of our present governmental theory ; and this being true, men of capacity and conscience would not throw their whole hearts and minds into a futile effort to patch up a theory that they believed could not stand. They would not violate their consciences, and peril their just reputations with posterity, by committing themselves to a position which they fully believed to be idle and false. Without claiming the slightest right to speak for the members of the bar, the simple opinion is given, that nine out of every ten have lost faith in our theory.

The following remarks of De Tocqueville upon the existing theory, will show what a distinguished foreigner, not unfriendly to our people, thinks of it :

" The Americans determined that the members of the Legislature should be elected by the people immediately, and for a very brief term, in order to subject them not only to the general convictions, but even to the daily passions of their constituents.

" When an individual or a party is wronged in the United States, to whom can he apply for redress ? If to public opinion, public opinion constitutes the majority ; if to the Legislature, it represents the majority, and implicitly obeys its instructions ; if to the executive power, it is appointed by the majority, and is a passive tool in its hands ; the public troops consist of the majority under arms ; the jury is the majority invested with the right of hearing judicial cases ; and in certain States even the judges are elected by the majority. However iniquitous or absurd the evil of which you complain may be, you must submit to it as well as you can."—(Pp. 275, 282.)

. Men, if they wish to govern, or be governed in peace and prosperity, must *themselves* be willing to submit to that which is just in itself. The mere passions and interested judgments both of majorities and minorities, must be restrained within proper limits. He who is in the majority to-day, and assists in opposing the minority, may to-morrow be in the minority, and be himself the victim. *There is no ground upon which all can meet, but that of justice.* But as men, for many reasons, differ as much as to what is just under certain circumstances as to any other questions, it becomes indispensable to have some authority to peacefully determine the controversy. All that a correct theory of government can do, is to provide tribunals that will not only act justly, but avoid even the appearance of injustice. Men will submit quietly, and even willingly, to the decisions of officers whose motives they are satisfied are pure. They will sooner forgive an error of judgment than a wilful wrong. When a theory of government is so constituted as to remove all temptation to do wrong by those in power, and thus leave no plausible ground for the imputation of interested or impure motives, it has done all that a theory of government can well do.

It is respectfully submitted, that the theory herein proposed will accomplish this. It is democratic, yet conservative—free, and yet not anarchical—strong, and yet not tyrannical. It is provided with ample checks upon abuses ; and yet every class in the nation can be heard in its councils. It proposes to secure the honesty of officers, by the simple and effectual method of removing the temptation to do wrong. Human virtue is always most secure in the absence of temptation.

There is a clear distinction between the Union and the existing Constitution. The first is of the utmost importance. Its permanent dissolution would be the greatest of political misfortunes; because it would, in its ultimate results, involve all other political evils. It would be better to have despotism with the Union, than despotism without it. The great Washington had every reason for his intense devotion to the Union. *"His devotion was a rational one."* And as to the Constitution, though defective, it should be *most faithfully* carried out, in its true spirit, until amended. Every violation of the Constitution is but a long step towards the utter and entire destruction of all theories of *limited governments*. It would be much better to submit patiently to any temporary evils arising from defects in the Constitution, rather than violate any of its provisions. Plain violations of that fundamental law, which all officers are sworn to support, are fatal precedents, alike destructive of public and private virtue.

We are now engaged in a terrible revolution, the precise termination of which no one can foresee. We can only speak of probabilities, not certainties. It is not probable that it will terminate in a permanent dissolution of the Union. It is most probable that there will be alternate successes and defeats on both sides, until both parties are well-nigh exhausted; and then they will be prepared to begin again at the beginning, and relay the foundation of our political edifice in a more practical and consistent theory of government. There is some danger that extreme exhaustion may hurry our people either into a despotism or a limited monarchy.* Men are prone to pass rapidly from one extreme to the other. But there is great reliance to be placed in the practical good sense of the American people. Trusting in that good sense, these views are submitted to their candid consideration.

---

* There is a plain distinction between a limited *monarchy* and a *government* of limited powers. The powers of the English *crown* are limited, and this makes it a limited monarchy. But the powers of that government itself are vested in the king and Parliament; and these, *taken together*, have no limits, except those of physical impossibility.

APPENDIX.

CONCERNING DANGERS FROM WAR BETWEEN THE STATES.

From the *Federalist*, No. VI. By ALEXANDER HAMILTON.

THE three last numbers of this work have been dedicated to an enumeration of the dangers to which we shall be exposed, in a state of disunion, from the arms and arts of foreign nations. I shall now proceed to delineate dangers of a different, and perhaps still more alarming kind; those which will, in all probability, flow from dissensions between the States themselves, and from domestic factions and convulsions. These have been already, in some instances, slightly anticipated; but they deserve a more particular and more full investigation.

If these States should either be wholly disunited, or only united in partial confederacies, a man must be far gone in Utopian speculations, who can seriously doubt that the subdivisions into which they might be thrown would have frequent and violent contests with each other. To presume a want of motives for such contests, as an argument against their existence, would be to forget that men are ambitious, vindictive, and rapacious. To look for a continuation of harmony between a number of independent, unconnected sovereignties, situated in the same neighborhood, would be to disregard the uniform course of human events, and to set at defiance the accumulated experience of ages.

The causes of hostility among nations are innumerable. There are some which have a general and almost constant operation upon the collective bodies of society. Of this description are the love of power, or the desire of preeminence and dominion—the jealousy of power, or the desire of equality and safety. There are others which have a more circumscribed, though an equally operative influence within their spheres; such are the rivalships and competitions of commerce between commercial nations. And there are others, not less numerous than either of the former, which take their origin entirely in private passions; in the attachments, enmities, interests, hopes, and fears of leading individuals in the communities of which they are members. Men of this class, whether the favorites of a king or of a people, have in too many instances abused the confidence they possessed; and, assuming the pretext of some public motive, have not scrupled to sacrifice the national tranquillity to personal advantage, or personal gratification.

The celebrated Pericles, in compliance with the resentment of a prostitute,* at the expense of much of the blood and treasure of his countrymen, attacked, vanquished, and destroyed the city of the *Samnians.* The same man, stimulated by private pique against the *Magarensians*, another nation of Greece, or to avoid a prosecution with which he was threatened as an accomplice in a supposed theft of the statuary *Phidias*, or to get rid of the accusations prepared to be brought against him for dissipating the funds of the state in the purchase of popularity, or from a combination of all these causes, was the primitive author of that famous and fatal war, distinguished in the Grecian annals by the name of the *Peloponnesian* war; which, after various vicissitudes, intermissions, and renewals, terminated in the ruin of the Athenian commonwealth.

The ambitious cardinal, who was prime minister to Henry VIII., permitting his vanity to aspire to the triple crown, entertained hopes of succeeding in the acquisition of that splended prize by the influence of the emperor Charles V. To secure the favor and interest of this enterprising and powerful monarch, he precipitated England into a war with France, contrary to the plainest dictates of policy, and at the hazard of the safety and independence, as well of the kingdom over which he presided by his counsels, as of Europe in general. For if there ever was a sovereign who bid fair to realize the project of universal monarchy, it was the emperor Charles V., of whose intrigues Wolsey was at once the instrument and the dupe.

The influence which the bigotry of one female,† the petulance of another,‡ and the cabals of a third,§ had in the cotemporary policy, ferments, and pacifications, of a considerable part of Europe, are topics that have been too often descanted upon not to be generally known.

To multiply examples of the agency of personal considerations in the production of great national events, either foreign or domestic, according to their direction, would be an unnecessary waste of time. Those who have but a superficial acquaintance with the sources from which they are to be drawn, will themselves recollect a variety of instances; and those who have a tolerable knowledge of human nature, will not stand in need of such lights, to form their opinion either of the reality or extent of that agency. Perhaps, however, a reference, tending to illustrate the general principle, may with propriety be made to a case which has lately happened among ourselves. If SHAYS had not been a *desperate debtor*, it is much to be doubted whether Massachusetts would have been plunged into a civil war.

But notwithstanding the concurring testimony of experience, in this particular, there are still to be found visionary or designing men, who stand ready to advocate the paradox of perpetual peace between the States, though dismembered and alienated from each other—the genius of republics, say they, is pacific; the spirit of commerce has a tendency to soften the manners·

---

* ASPASIA : vide PLUTARCH's life of Pericles.
† Madame de Maintenon.   ‡ Duchess of Marlborough.
                   § Madame de Pompadour.

of men, and to extinguish those inflammable humors which have so often kindled into wars. Commercial republics, like ours, will never be disposed to waste themselves in ruinous contentions with each other. They will be governed by mutual interest, and will cultivate a spirit of mutual amity and concord.

We may ask these projectors in politics, whether it is not the true interest of all nations to cultivate the same benevolent and philosophic spirit? If this be their true interest, have they, in fact, pursued it? Has it not, on the contrary, invariably been found that momentary passions, and immediate interests, have a more active and imperious control over human conduct than general or remote considerations of policy, utility, or justice? Have republics in practice been less addicted to war than monarchies? Are not the former administered by men as well as the latter? Are there not aversions, predilections, rivalships, and desires of unjust acquisition, that affect nations as well as kings? Are not popular assemblies frequently subject to the impulses of rage, resentment, jealousy, avarice, and of other irregular and violent propensities? Is it not well known, that their determinations are often governed by a few individuals in whom they place confidence, and that they are, of course, liable to be tinctured by the passions and views of those individuals? Has commerce hitherto done any thing more than changed the objects of war? Is not the love of wealth as domineering and enterprising a passion as that of power or glory? Have there not been as many wars founded upon commercial motives, since that has become the prevailing system of nations, as were before occasioned by the cupidity of territory or dominion? Has not the spirit of commerce, in many instances, administered new incentives to the appetite, both for the one and for the other? Let experience, the least fallible guide of human opinions, be appealed to for an answer to these inquiries.

Sparta, Athens, Rome, and Carthage, were all republics; two of them, Athens and Carthage, of the commercial kind. Yet were they as often engaged in wars, offensive and defensive, as the neighboring monarchies of the same times. Sparta was little better than a well-regulated camp; and Rome was never sated of carnage and conquest.

Carthage, though a commercial republic, was the aggressor, in the very war that ended in her destruction. Hannibal had carried her arms into the heart of Italy, and even to the gates of Rome, before Scipio, in turn, gave him an overthrow in the territories of Carthage, and made a conquest of the commonwealth.

Venice, in latter times, figured more than once in wars of ambition; till, becoming an object of terror to the other Italian states, Pope Julius the Second found means to accomplish that formidable league,* which gave a deadly blow to the power and pride of that haughty republic.

The provinces of Holland, till they were overwhelmed in debts and taxes, took a leading and conspicuous part in the wars of Europe. They had furious

---

* The LEAGUE OF CAMBRAY, comprehending the emperor, the King of France, the King of Arragon, and most of the Italian princes and States.

contests with England for the dominion of the sea; and were among the most persevering and most implacable of the opponents of Louis XIV.

In the government of Britain the representatives of the people compose one branch of the national legislature. Commerce has been for ages the predominant pursuit of that country. Yet few nations have been more frequently engaged in war; and the wars in which that kingdom has been engaged, have in numerous instances proceeded from the people. There have been, if I may so express it, almost as many popular as royal wars. The cries of the nation and the importunities of their representatives have, upon various occasions, dragged their monarchs into war, or continued them in it, contrary to their inclinations, and sometimes contrary to the real interests of the State. In that memorable struggle for superiority between the rival houses of *Austria* and *Bourbon*, which so long kept Europe in a flame, it is well known that the antipathies of the English against the French, seconding the ambition, or rather the avarice of a favorite leader,* protracted the war beyond the limits marked out by sound policy, and for a considerable time in opposition to the views of the court.

The wars of these two last-mentioned nations have in a great measure grown out of commercial considerations; the desire of supplanting, and the fear of being supplanted, either in particular branches of traffic, or in the general advantages of trade and navigation; and sometimes even the more culpable desire of sharing in the commerce of other nations, without their consent.

The last war but two between Britain and Spain sprang from the attempts of the English merchants to prosecute an illicit trade with the Spanish main. These unjustifiable practices, on their part, produced severities on the part of the Spaniards towards the subjects of Great Britain, which were not more justifiable; because they exceeded the bounds of a just retaliation and were chargeable with inhumanity and cruelty. Many of the English who were taken on the Spanish coasts were sent to dig in the mines of Potosi; and, by the usual progress of a spirit of resentment, the innocent were after a while confounded with the guilty in indiscriminate punishment. The complaints of the merchants kindled a violent flame throughout the nation, which soon after broke out in the House of Commons and was communicated from that body to the Ministry. Letters of reprisal were granted, and a war ensued, which, in its consequences, overthrew all the alliances that but twenty years before had been formed, with sanguine expectations of the most beneficial fruits.

From this summary of what has taken place in other countries, whose situations have borne the nearest resemblance to our own, what reason can we have to confide in those reveries which would seduce us into the expectation of peace and cordiality between the members of the present confederacy in a state of separation? Have we not already seen enough of the fallacy and extravagance of those idle theories which have amused us with promises of an exemption from the imperfections, the weaknesses, and the evils incident to society in every shape? Is it not time to awake from the deceitful

* The Duke of Marlborough.

dream of a golden age, and to adopt as a practical maxim for the direction of our political conduct, that we, as well as the other inhabitants of the globe, are yet remote from the happy empire of perfect wisdom and perfect virtue?

Let the point of extreme depression to which our national dignity and credit have sunk; let the inconveniences felt everywhere from a lax and ill-administration of Government; let the revolt of a part of the State of North Carolina; the late menacing disturbances in Pennsylvania, and the actual insurrections and rebellions in Massachusetts, declare!

So far is the general sense of mankind from corresponding with the tenets of those who endeavor to lull asleep our apprehensions of discord and hostility between the States, in the event of disunion, that it has from long observation of the progress of society become a sort of axiom in politics, that vicinity or nearness of situation constitutes nations natural enemies. An intelligent writer expresses himself on this subject to this effect : "NEIGHBORING NATIONS (says he) are naturally ENEMIES of each other, unless their common weakness forces them to league in a CONFEDERATIVE REPUBLIC, and their constitution prevents the differences that neighborhood occasions, extinguishing that secret jealousy which disposes all States to aggrandize themselves at the expense of their neighbors."* This passage, at the same time, points out the EVIL, and suggests the REMEDY.   PUBLIUS.

THE EFFECTS OF INTERNAL WAR IN PRODUCING STANDING ARMIES, AND OTHER INSTITUTIONS UNFRIENDLY TO LIBERTY.

From the *Federalist*, No. VIII. By ALEXANDER HAMILTON.

ASSUMING it therefore as an established truth, that, in case of disunion, the several States, or such combinations of them as might happen to be formed out of the wreck of the general confederacy, would be subject to those vicissitudes of peace and war, of friendship and enmity with each other, which have fallen to the lot of all neighboring nations not united under one government, let us enter into a concise detail of some of the consequences that would attend such a situation.

War between the States, in the first periods of their separate existence, would be accompanied with much greater distresses than it commonly is in those countries where regular military establishments have long obtained. The disciplined armies always kept on foot on the continent of Europe, though they bear a malignant aspect to liberty and economy, have, notwithstanding, been productive of the signal advantage of rendering sudden conquests impracticable, and of preventing that rapid desolation which used to mark the progress of war prior to their introduction. The art of fortification has contributed to the same ends. The nations of Europe are encircled with chains

* Vide Principles des Negotiations par l'Abbe de Mably.

of fortified places, which mutually obstruct invasion. Campaigns are wasted in reducing two or three frontier garrisons, to gain admittance into an enemy's country. Similar impediments occur at every step, to exhaust the strength and delay the progress of an invader. Formerly an invading army would penetrate into the heart of a neighboring country, almost as soon as intelligence of its approach could be received; but now, a comparatively small force of disciplined troops, acting on the defensive, with the aid of posts, is able to impede, and finally to frustrate, the enterprises of one much more considerable. The history of war in that quarter of the globe is no longer a history of nations subdued and empires overturned; but of towns taken and retaken, of battles that decide nothing, of retreats more beneficial than victories, of much effort and little acquisition.

In this country, the scene would be altogether reversed. The jealousy of military establishments, would postpone them as long as possible. The want of fortifications, leaving the frontiers of one State open to another, would facilitate inroads. The populous States would, with little difficulty, overrun their less populous neighbors. Conquests would be as easy to be made, as difficult to be retained. War, therefore, would be desultory and predatory. Plunder and devastation ever march in the train of irregulars. The calamities of individuals would make the principal figure in the events which would characterize our military exploits.

This picture is not too highly wrought; though, I confess, it would not long remain a just one. Safety from external danger is the most powerful director of national conduct. Even the ardent love of liberty will, after a time, give way to its dictates. The violent destruction of life and property, incident to war; the continual effort and alarm attendant on a state of continual danger, will compel nations.the most attached to liberty, to resort for repose and security to' institutions which have a tendency to destroy their civil and political rights. To be more safe, they at length become willing to run the risk of being less free.

The institutions chiefly alluded to are STANDING ARMIES, and the correspondent appendages of military establishments. Standing armies, it is said, are not provided against in the new constitution; and it is thence inferred that they would exist under it.* This inference, from the very form of the proposition, is, at best, problematical and uncertain. But STANDING ARMIES, it may be replied, must inevitably result from a dissolution of the confederacy. Frequent war, and constant apprehension, which require a state of as constant preparation, will infallibly produce them. The weaker States, or confederacies, would first have recourse to them, to put themselves upon an equality with their more potent neighbors. They would endeavor to supply the inferiority of population and resources by a more regular and effective system of defence, by disciplined troops, and by fortifications. They would, at the same time, be obliged to strengthen the executive arm of government : in doing which, their constitutions would acquire a progressive direction

* This objection will be fully examined in its proper place; and it will be shown that the only rational precaution which could have been taken on this subject, has been taken; and a much better one than is to be found in any constitution that has been heretofore framed in America, most of which contain no guard at all on this subject.

towards monarchy. It is of the nature of war to increase the executive, at the expense of the legislative authority.

The expedients which have been mentioned would soon give the States, or confederacies, that made use of them, a superiority over their neighbors. Small States, or States of less natural strength, under vigorous governments, and with the assistance of disciplined armies, have often triumphed over large States, or States of greater natural strength, which have been destitute of these advantages. Neither the pride, nor the safety, of the more important States, or confederacies, would permit them long to submit to this mortifying and adventitious superiority. They would quickly resort to means similar to those by which it had been effected, to reinstate themselves in their lost pre-eminence. Thus we should, in a little time, see established, in every part of this country, the same engines of despotism which have been the scourge of the old world. This, at least, would be the natural course of things; and our reasonings will be likely to be just, in proportion as they are accommodated to this standard.

These are not vague inferences deduced from speculative defects in a constitution, the whole power of which is lodged in the hands of the people, or their representatives and delegates; they are solid conclusions, drawn from the natural and necessary progress of human affairs.

It may perhaps be asked, by way of objection, why did not standing armies spring up out of the contentions which so often distracted the ancient republics of Greece? Different answers, equally satisfactory, may be given to this question. The industrious habits of the people of the present day, absorbed in the pursuits of gain, and devoted to the improvements of agriculture and commerce, are incompatible with the condition of a nation of soldiers, which was the true condition of the people of those republics. The means of revenue, which have been so greatly multiplied by the increase of gold and silver, and of the arts of industry and of the science of finance, which is the offspring of modern times, concurring with the habits of nations, have produced an entire revolution in the system of war, and have rendered disciplined armies, distinct from the body of the citizens, the inseparable companion of frequent hostility.

There is a wide difference, also, between military establishments in a country which, by its situation, is seldom exposed to invasions, and in one which is often subject to them, and always apprehensive of them. The rulers of the former can have no good pretext, if they are even so inclined, to keep on foot armies so numerous as must of necessity be maintained in the latter. These armies being, in the first case, rarely, if at all, called into activity for interior defence, the people are in no danger of being broken to military subordination. The laws are not accustomed to relaxations in favor of military exigencies; the civil state remains in full vigor, neither corrupted, nor confounded with the principles or propensities of the other State. The smallness of the army forbids competition with the natural strength of the community, and the citizens, not habituated to look up to the military power for protection, or to submit to its oppressions, neither love nor fear the soldiery: they view them with a spirit of jealous acquiescence in a necessary evil, and stand ready to resist a power which they suppose may be exerted to the prejudice of their rights.

The army, under such circumstances, though it may usefully aid the magistrate to suppress a small faction, or an occasional mob, or insurrection, will be utterly incompetent to the purpose of enforcing encroachments against the united efforts of the great body of the people.

But in a country where the perpetual menacings of danger oblige the government to be always prepared to repel it, her armies must be numerous enough for instant defence. The continual necessity for his services enhances the importance of the soldier, and proportionably degrades the condition of the citizen. The military state becomes elevated above the civil. The inhabitants of territories often the theatre of war, are unavoidably subjected to frequent infringements on their rights, which serve to weaken their sense of those rights; and by degrees the people are brought to consider the soldiery not only as their protectors, but as their superiors. The transition from this disposition to that of considering them as masters is neither remote nor difficult: but it is very difficult to prevail upon a people under such impressions to make a bold or effectual resistance to usurpations supported by the military power.

The kingdom of Great Britain falls within the first description. An insular situation, and a powerful marine, guarding it in a great measure against the possibility of foreign invasion, supersede the necessity of a numerous army within the kingdom. A sufficient force to make head against a sudden descent till the militia could have time to rally and embody, is all that has been deemed requisite. No motive of national policy has demanded, nor would public opinion have tolerated, a larger number of troops upon its domestic establishment. This peculiar felicity of situation has, in a great degree, contributed to preserve the liberty which that country to this day enjoys, in spite of the prevalent venality and corruption. If Britain had been situated on the continent, and had been compelled, as she would have been, by that situation, to make her military establishments at home coextensive with those of the other great powers of Europe, she, like them, would, in all probability, at this day, be a victim to the absolute power of a single man. It is possible, though not easy, for the people of that island to be enslaved from other causes; but it cannot be by the prowess of an army so inconsiderable as that which has been usually kept up within the kingdom.

If we are wise enough to preserve the Union, we may for ages enjoy an advantage similar to that of an insulated situation. Europe is at a great distance from us. Her colonies in our vicinity will be likely to continue too much disproportionate in strength, to be able to give us any dangerous annoyance. Extensive military establishments cannot, in this position, be necessary to our security. But if we should be disunited, and the integral parts should either remain separated, or, which is most probable, should be thrown together into two or three confederacies, we should be, in a short course of time, in the predicament of the continental powers of Europe. Our liberties would be a prey to the means of defending ourselves against the ambition and jealousy of each other.

This is an idea not superficial nor futile, but solid and weighty. It deserves the most serious and mature consideration of every prudent and honest man, of whatever party : if such men will make a firm and solemn pause, and meditate dispassionately on its vast importance ; if they will contemplate it in all its attitudes, and trace it to all its consequences, they will not hesitate to part with trivial objections to a constitution, the rejection of which would in all probability put a final period to the Union. The airy phantoms that now flit before the distempered imaginations of some of its adversaries, would then quickly give place to the more substantial prospects of dangers, real, certain, and extremely formidable. PUBLIUS.

THE END.

www.ingramcontent.com/pod-product-compliance
Lightning Source LLC
Chambersburg PA
CBHW021414090426
42742CB00009B/1140